A YEAR IN ARCHITECTURE

CLAUDIA STÄUBLE AND JONATHAN LEE FOX

PRESTEL

MUNICH | BERLIN | LONDON | NEW YORK

In cooperation with  agentur für **laif** photos & reportagen

© Prestel Verlag, Munich · Berlin · London · New York 2009

© for all images by laif 2009
Photo credits see last page

© of works illustrated by the architects, their heirs or assigns with
the exception of: Santiago Calatrava, Walter Gropius, Rem Koolhaas,
Mies van der Rohe and Frank Lloyd Wright bei VG Bild-Kunst, Bonn 2009;
Le Corbusier by FLC/VG Bild-Kunst, Bonn 2009

Cover: William van Alen, Chrysler Building, New York (Christian Heeb for laif)

Prestel Verlag
Königinstraße 9, 80539 Munich
Tel. +49 (89) 24 29 08 300
Fax +49 (89) 24 29 08 335

Prestel Publishing Ltd.
4, Bloomsbury Place, London WC1A 2QA
Tel. +44 (20) 7323-5004
Fax +44 (20) 7636-8004

Prestel Publishing
900 Broadway, Suite 603
New York, N.Y. 10003
Tel. +1 (212) 995-2720
Fax +1 (212) 995-2733
www.prestel.com

Library of Congress Control Number: 2009928340

British Library Cataloguing-in-Publication Data
A catalogue record for this book is available from the British Library.

The Deutsche Bibliothek holds a record for this publication in the Deutsche
Nationalbibliografie; detailed biographical data can be found under:
http://dnb.ddb.de

Prestel books are available worldwide. Please contact your nearest bookseller or
one of the listed addresses for information concerning your local distributor.

Editorial direction by Claudia Stäuble
Editorial assistance by Rahel Goldner
Quotes compilation by Jonathan Lee Fox
Cover and layout concept by LIQUID, Augsburg
Production by Astrid Wedemeyer
Typesetting by Vornehm, Munich
Origination by ReproLine Mediateam
Printing and binding by C&C JOINT PRINTING CO. Ltd., Shanghai

Printed on acid-free paper

ISBN: 978-3-7913-4228-3

When we build let us think
we build forever.

John Ruskin

We may live without her, and worship
without her, but we cannot remember
without her. How cold is all history,
how lifeless all imagery, compared
to that which the living nation writes,
and the uncorrupted marble bears!

John Ruskin

Taj Mahal, 1631–1648
Agra/India

1 2 3 4 5 6 7 8 9 10 11 12 13 14 15 16 17 18 19 20 21 22 23 24 25 26 27 28 29 30 31

JANUARY

I believe that to be really modern,
architecture has to carry some
archaic, historical values.

Mario Botta

San Francisco Museum of Modern Art, 1994
Mario Botta
San Francisco/USA

1 2 3 4 5 6 7 8 9 10 11 12 13 14 15 16 17 18 19 20 21 22 23 24 25 26 27 28 29 30 31

JANUARY

The love of learning,
the sequestered nooks,
And all the sweet serenity of books.

Henry Wadsworth Longfellow

The Glasgow School of Art, Library, 1897–1909
Charles Rennie Mackintosh
Glasgow/Scotland

1 2 3 4 5 6 7 8 9 10 11 12 13 14 15 16 17 18 19 20 21 22 23 24 25 26 27 28 29 30 31

JANUARY

Pure holy simplicity confounds
all the wisdom of this world
and the wisdom of the flesh.

St. Francis of Assisi

Monastery Church of Santa Maria del Patire, 1100
Rossano/Italy

1 2 3 4 5 6 7 8 9 10 11 12 13 14 15 16 17 18 19 20 21 22 23 24 25 26 27 28 29 30 31

JANUARY

It is a feeling which he would like
to call a sensation of "eternity,"
a feeling as of something limitless,
unbounded – as it were, "oceanic."

Sigmund Freud

L'Hôtel de Cluny, 1485–1490
Paris/France

1 2 3 4 5 6 7 8 9 10 11 12 13 14 15 16 17 18 19 20 21 22 23 24 25 26 27 28 29 30 31

JANUARY

Unless he enter the gate,
no man can see the beauty
of the Ancestral Temples,
the wealth of the hundred officers.

Confucius

Forbidden City, gate path, 1406–1420
Beijing/China

1 2 3 4 5 **6** 7 8 9 10 11 12 13 14 15 16 17 18 19 20 21 22 23 24 25 26 27 28 29 30 31

JANUARY

As the management of light is a
matter of importance in architecture,
it is worth inquiring, how far this remark
is applicable to building. I think then,
that all edifices calculated to produce
an idea of the sublime, ought rather to
be dark and gloomy.

Edmund Burke

Basilica San Lorenzo, ceiling vault, 1666–1679
Guarino Guarini
Turin, Italy

1 2 3 4 5 6 **7** 8 9 10 11 12 13 14 15 16 17 18 19 20 21 22 23 24 25 26 27 28 29 30 31

JANUARY

Art must make use of its resources to
embellish, smooth and polish the
work without touching the substance
of the plan.

Marc-Antoine Laugier

Villa Tugendhat, 1930
Ludwig Mies van der Rohe
Brno/Czech Republic

1 2 3 4 5 6 7 **8** 9 10 11 12 13 14 15 16 17 18 19 20 21 22 23 24 25 26 27 28 29 30 31

JANUARY

Architecture is the will of an epoch
translated into space.

Ludwig Mies van der Rohe

Empire State Building, 1930–1931
Shreve, Lamb & Harmon
New York/USA

1 2 3 4 5 6 7 8 **9** 10 11 12 13 14 15 16 17 18 19 20 21 22 23 24 25 26 27 28 29 30 31

JANUARY

Before I go further, however, I think
I should explain exactly whom I mean
by architect: for it is no carpenter
that I would have you compare to the
greatest exponents of other disciplines;
the carpenter is but an instrument
in the hands of the architect.

Leon Battista Alberti

Jefferson Memorial, 1939–1943
John Russell Pope
Washington, DC/USA

1 2 3 4 5 6 7 8 9 **10** 11 12 13 14 15 16 17 18 19 20 21 22 23 24 25 26 27 28 29 30 31

JANUARY

The will to do, the soul to dare.

Sir Walter Scott

Millau Viaduct, 2001–2004
Michel Virlogeux, Norman Foster
Millau/France

1 2 3 4 5 6 7 8 9 10 **11** 12 13 14 15 16 17 18 19 20 21 22 23 24 25 26 27 28 29 30 31

JANUARY

Poetry must be new as foam,
and as old as the rock.

Ralph Waldo Emerson

Sainte-Marie de la Tourette, 1956–1960
Le Corbusier
Éveux/France

1 2 3 4 5 6 7 8 9 10 11 12 13 14 15 16 17 18 19 20 21 22 23 24 25 26 27 28 29 30 31

JANUARY

I believe the right question to ask,
respecting all ornament, is simply this:
Was it done with enjoyment – was the
carver happy while he was about it?

John Ruskin

Mezquita of Cordoba, wall detail, 600–987
Cordoba/Spain

1 2 3 4 5 6 7 8 9 10 11 12 **13** 14 15 16 17 18 19 20 21 22 23 24 25 26 27 28 29 30 31

JANUARY

It's very difficult to explain why you do things,
why you curve something. It becomes an
evolution of thought and ideas. I feel like the
picture of the cat pushing the ball of string.
You just keep pushing it and it moves around.
Then it falls off the table and creates this
beautiful line in space.

Frank O. Gehry

Cinémathèque Française, 1994
Frank O. Gehry
Paris/France

1 2 3 4 5 6 7 8 9 10 11 12 13 14 15 16 17 18 19 20 21 22 23 24 25 26 27 28 29 30 31

JANUARY

Intelligence is
not to make no mistakes
But quickly to see
how to make them good.

Bertolt Brecht

Cathedral of Pisa (Santa Maria Assunta) with the Leaning Tower, 1063–1372
Pisa/Italy

1 2 3 4 5 6 7 8 9 10 11 12 13 14 **15** 16 17 18 19 20 21 22 23 24 25 26 27 28 29 30 31

JANUARY

Prada and Beijing are perhaps
our most perfect designs to date.
The similarity is that in both cases
is that there is no structure, there is
no façade, there is no space,
there is no ornamentation.

Jacques Herzog

Prada Store Aoyama, 2001–2003
Herzog & de Meuron
Tokyo/Japan

1 2 3 4 5 6 7 8 9 10 11 12 13 14 15 16 17 18 19 20 21 22 23 24 25 26 27 28 29 30 31

JANUARY

PRADA

AOYAMA/H&deM/JUNE 7 2003

God needs us. We are the grains
of sand in the bricks with which he
constructs the history of humanity.

Friedrich Naumann

Basilica St. Sernin, portal capitals, 1077–1119
Toulouse/France

1 2 3 4 5 6 7 8 9 10 11 12 13 14 15 16 17 18 19 20 21 22 23 24 25 26 27 28 29 30 31

JANUARY

Music assists him in the use of harmonic and mathematical proportion.

Vitruvius

Ciudad de las Artes y de las Ciencias (City of Arts and Sciences), 1991–2006
Santiago Calatrava
Valencia/Spain

1 2 3 4 5 6 7 8 9 10 11 12 13 14 15 16 17 18 19 20 21 22 23 24 25 26 27 28 29 30 31

JANUARY

The pavement of the church is
the foundation of our faith. But in
the spiritual Church, the pavement is
the poor of Christ: the poor in spirit,
who humble themselves in all things.

William Durandus

Amiens Cathedral (Notre-Dame d'Amiens), nave labyrinth, after 1218
Robert de Luzarches et al.
Amiens/France

1 2 3 4 5 6 7 8 9 10 11 12 13 14 15 16 17 18 19 20 21 22 23 24 25 26 27 28 29 30 31

JANUARY

Architecture is not just about making
good buildings … it's also about telling
stories in some way.

Renzo Piano

New York Times Building, staircase, 2003–2007
Renzo Piano
New York/USA

1 2 3 4 5 6 7 8 9 10 11 12 13 14 15 16 17 18 19 20 21 22 23 24 25 26 27 28 29 30 31

JANUARY

Believe me, that was a happy age,
before the days of architects,
before the days of builders.

Seneca

1 2 3 4 5 6 7 8 9 10 11 12 13 14 15 16 17 18 19 20 21 22 23 24 25 26 27 28 29 30 31

JANUARY

What is originality? That's the question
there. To be original is not the most
important thing is it? I mean to design
something you have to know
that this is the best you can do
for that particular circumstance,
not always the most original.

I. M. Pei

Wembley Stadium, 2003–2007
Norman Foster
London/England

1 2 3 4 5 6 7 8 9 10 11 12 13 14 15 16 17 18 19 20 21 22 23 24 25 26 27 28 29 30 31

JANUARY

Silence is as full of potential wisdom
and wit as the unhewn marble of
great sculpture.

Aldous Huxley

Abbey of Saint-Pierre, 1059–1131
Moissac/France

1 2 3 4 5 6 7 8 9 10 11 12 13 14 15 16 17 18 19 20 21 22 23 24 25 26 27 28 29 30 31

JANUARY

The concept of tectonics links the
seemingly antagonistic spheres of
art and technology in architecture.

Hans Kollhoff

Potsdamer Platz with Bahn Tower, 1998–2000
Helmut Jahn
Berlin/Germany

1 2 3 4 5 6 7 8 9 10 11 12 13 14 15 16 17 18 19 20 21 22 23 24 25 26 27 28 29 30 31

JANUARY

A beautiful architectural monument
has not any determinate meaning,
if it may be so expressed, so that we
are seized, in contemplating it, with
that kind of aimless reverie, which leads
us into a boundless ocean of thought.

Madame de Staël

Cathedral of Brixen (Bressanone), 1745
Bressanone/Italy

1 2 3 4 5 6 7 8 9 10 11 12 13 14 15 16 17 18 19 20 21 22 23 24 25 26 27 28 29 30 31

JANUARY

By night the skyscraper looms in the
smoke and the stars and has a soul.

Chrysler Building, 1928–1930
William van Alen
New York/USA

Carl Sandburg

1 2 3 4 5 6 7 8 9 10 11 12 13 14 15 16 17 18 19 20 21 22 23 24 25 26 27 28 29 30 31

JANUARY

Architecture, of all the arts,
is the one which acts the most slowly,
but the most surely, on the soul.

Ernest Dimnet

Cathedral of Seville (Santa María de la Sede), transept façade, ca. 1517
Seville/Spain

1 2 3 4 5 6 7 8 9 10 11 12 13 14 15 16 17 18 19 20 21 22 23 24 25 26 27 28 29 30 31

JANUARY

The unusual only has value
if there is something like ordinariness.

Peter Eisenman

City Hall, Greater London Authority, 2000–2002
Norman Foster & Partner
London/England

1 2 3 4 5 6 7 8 9 10 11 12 13 14 15 16 17 18 19 20 21 22 23 24 25 26 27 28 29 30 31

JANUARY

The way of humility is good,
for by it we seek truth, attain love,
and share the fruits of wisdom.

Bernard of Clairvaux

Church of Agios Vasilios, end of the 14th century
Arta/Greece

1 2 3 4 5 6 7 8 9 10 11 12 13 14 15 16 17 18 19 20 21 22 23 24 25 26 27 28 29 30 31

JANUARY

All journeys have secret destinations
of which the traveler is unaware.

Martin Buber

Gare Lyon-Saint-Exupéry, 1994
Santiago Calatrava
Lyon/France

1 2 3 4 5 6 7 8 9 10 11 12 13 14 15 16 17 18 19 20 21 22 23 24 25 26 27 28 29 30 31

JANUARY

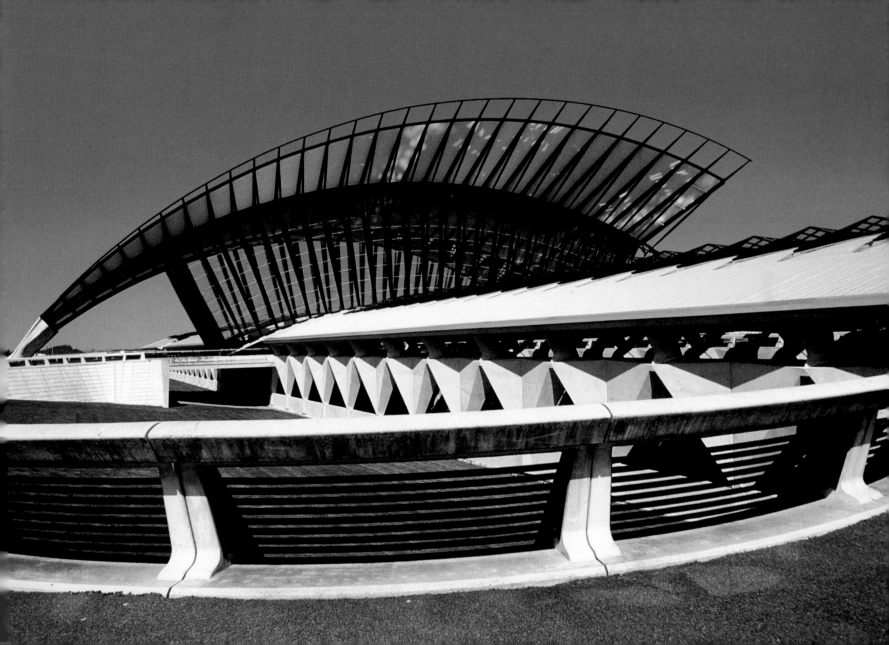

The form is not the goal
but the result of our work.

Ludwig Mies van der Rohe

Notre-Dame du Haut, 1955
Le Corbusier
Ronchamp/France

1
2 3 4 5 6 7 8 9 10 11 12 13 14 15 16 17 18 19 20 21 22 23 24 25 26 27 28/29

FEBRUARY

The universal edifice he praises
And shows it off as symmetry.

Friedrich von Schiller

Royal Saltworks, 1775–1778
Claude Nicolas Ledoux
Arc-et-Senans/France

1 2 3 4 5 6 7 8 9 10 11 12 13 14 15 16 17 18 19 20 21 22 23 24 25 26 27 28/29

FEBRUARY

I find myself drawn to explore what I call the void – the presence of an overwhelming emptiness created when a community is wiped out, or individual freedom is stamped out; when the continuity of life is so brutally disrupted that the structure of life is forever torqued and transformed.

Daniel Libeskind

Jewish Museum Berlin, 1992–2001
Daniel Libeskind
Berlin/Germany

3

1 2 3 4 5 6 7 8 9 10 11 12 13 14 15 16 17 18 19 20 21 22 23 24 25 26 27 28/29

FEBRUARY

Is it not certain that the Creator yawns
in earthquake and thunder and other
popular displays, but toils in rounding
the delicate spiral of a shell?

William Butler Yeats

Melk Benedictine Abbey, spiral staircase, 1725–1750
Jakob Prandtauer, Josef Munggenast
Melk/Austria

1 2 3 4 5 6 7 8 9 10 11 12 13 14 15 16 17 18 19 20 21 22 23 24 25 26 27 28/29

FEBRUARY

I am certain that a multiplicity of
ornaments will not present to the eye
a confusion of objects, but a graceful
and pleasing disposition of things.

Giovanni Battista Piranesi

Ornamental gables of gilded houses on Brussels' Grand Place, ca. 1700
Brussels/Belgium

1 2 3 4 5 6 7 8 9 10 11 12 13 14 15 16 17 18 19 20 21 22 23 24 25 26 27 28/29

FEBRUARY

While the main concern inside the
museum is to create ideal exhibiting
conditions, its exterior is designed
to draw attention to its role as
a receptacle of living art:
the polychrome façade looks
like a large abstract painting.

Louisa Hutton, Matthias Sauerbruch

Museum Brandhorst, 2008
sauerbruch hutton
Munich/Germany

1 2 3 4 5 **6** 7 8 9 10 11 12 13 14 15 16 17 18 19 20 21 22 23 24 25 26 27 28/29

FEBRUARY

Our guiding principle is function, utility our first
condition, our strength must lie in good
proportions and the proper treatment of
material. We shall seek to decorate when it
seems required but we do not fell obliged to
adorn at any price.

Josef Hoffmann

Bauhaus building, façade detail, 1925–1926
Walter Gropius
Dessau/Germany

1 2 3 4 5 6 7 8 9 10 11 12 13 14 15 16 17 18 19 20 21 22 23 24 25 26 27 28/29

FEBRUARY

All art, therefore, appeals primarily to the senses, and the artistic aim when expressing itself in written words must also make its appeal through the senses, if its high desire is to reach the secret spring of responsive emotions.

Joseph Conrad

Kalyan Mosque, 1514
Bukhara/Uzbekistan

1 2 3 4 5 6 7 8 9 10 11 12 13 14 15 16 17 18 19 20 21 22 23 24 25 26 27 28/29

FEBRUARY

Opposition brings concord. Out of
discord comes the fairest harmony.

Heraclitus

Berlin Philharmonic, 1960–1963
Hans Scharoun
Berlin/Germany

1 2 3 4 5 6 7 8 9 **10** 11 12 13 14 15 16 17 18 19 20 21 22 23 24 25 26 27 28/29

FEBRUARY

The activity of art is based on the fact
that a man, receiving through his
sense of hearing or sight another
man's expression of feeling, is capable
of experiencing the emotion which
moved the man who expressed it.

Leo Tolstoy

Church of the Holy Spirit, 1407–1461
Hans von Burghausen
Landshut/Germany

1 2 3 4 5 6 7 8 9 10 **11** 12 13 14 15 16 17 18 19 20 21 22 23 24 25 26 27 28/29

FEBRUARY

Architecture is more than sculpture or
the means of giving pure expression
to abstract human ideals. Our visual
world is determined by "forces" of
a practical nature, not only by the
unique contribution of true artists.

Pietro Belluschi

Elne Cathedral (Sainte-Eulalie-et-Sainte-Julie), cloister capital, 12th–14th century
Elne/France

1 2 3 4 5 6 7 8 9 10 11 12 13 14 15 16 17 18 19 20 21 22 23 24 25 26 27 28/29

FEBRUARY

Divine nature gave the fields,
human art built the cities.

Marcus Terentius Varro

World Financial Center, 1985–1988
César Pelli
New York/USA

1 2 3 4 5 6 7 8 9 10 11 12 **13** 14 15 16 17 18 19 20 21 22 23 24 25 26 27 28/29

FEBRUARY

To be conscious is not to be in time

But only in time can the moment in the rosegarden,

The moment in the arbour where the rain beat,

The moment in the draughty church at smokefall.

Be remembered; involved with past and future,

Only through time time is conquered.

T. S. Eliot

Temple of Confucius, 1285
Jianshui/China

1 2 3 4 5 6 7 8 9 10 11 12 13 14 15 16 17 18 19 20 21 22 23 24 25 26 27 28/29

FEBRUARY

The sums of interrelationships of all
the experiences of each of our lives
are always tetrahedronal, and all the
relationships of all the component
events of the universe are always
tetrahedronal.

Buckminster Fuller

Pyramids of Giza, 2620–2500 BCE
Giza/Egypt

1 2 3 4 5 6 7 8 9 10 11 12 13 14 15 16 17 18 19 20 21 22 23 24 25 26 27 28/29

FEBRUARY

As every one knows, meditation
and water are wedded forever.

Herman Melville

Torre del Agua (Water Tower), 2008
Enrique de Teresa
Zaragoza/Spain

1 2 3 4 5 6 7 8 9 10 11 12 13 14 15 **16** 17 18 19 20 21 22 23 24 25 26 27 28/29

FEBRUARY

First were the thick stone walls,
the arches, then the domes
and vaults – of the architect,
searching out for wider spaces.

Oscar Niemeyer

Santa Maria in Roa, ceiling vault, 16th century
Roa/Spain

1 2 3 4 5 6 7 8 9 10 11 12 13 14 15 16 **17** 18 19 20 21 22 23 24 25 26 27 28/29

FEBRUARY

An Architect ought to be jealous
of Novelties, in which Fancy
blinds the Judgment; and to think
his Judges, as well those that are
to live five Centuries after him,
as those of his own Time.

Christopher Wren

St. Paul's Cathedral, 1675–1708
Christopher Wren
London/England

1 2 3 4 5 6 7 8 9 10 11 12 13 14 15 16 17 **18** 19 20 21 22 23 24 25 26 27 28/29

FEBRUARY

Men achieve tranquility through
moderation in pleasure and
through the symmetry of life.

Democritus

Sera Monastery, 1970
Kushalnagar/India

1 2 3 4 5 6 7 8 9 10 11 12 13 14 15 16 17 18 19 20 21 22 23 24 25 26 27 28/29

FEBRUARY

Art is harmony. Harmony is the analogy
of contrary and of similar elements of
tone, of color and of line.

Georges Seurat

Kurjey Lhakhang (monastery), detail, after 1652
Bumthang/Bhutan

1 2 3 4 5 6 7 8 9 10 11 12 13 14 15 16 17 18 19 20 21 22 23 24 25 26 27 28/29

FEBRUARY

The architect represents neither a
Dionysian nor an Apollonian state:
here it is the great act of will,
the will which removes mountains,
the intoxication of the great will,
that is demanding to become art.

Friedrich Nietzsche

Neuschwanstein Castle, 1869–1884
Eduard Riedel, Christian Jank
Schwangau/Germany

1 2 3 4 5 6 7 8 9 10 11 12 13 14 15 16 17 18 19 20 21 22 23 24 25 26 27 28/29

FEBRUARY

Architecture is the printing-press of all
ages, and gives a history of the state of
the society in which it was erected.

Lady Morgan

Alcázar of Seville, Courtyard of the Maidens, 1364
Seville/Spain

1 2 3 4 5 6 7 8 9 10 11 12 13 14 15 16 17 18 19 20 21 22 23 24 25 26 27 28/29

FEBRUARY

As ornament is no longer organically related to our culture, it is also no longer the expression of our culture.

Adolf Loos

Medina Azahara, detail, 936–976
Cordoba/Spain

1 2 3 4 5 6 7 8 9 10 11 12 13 14 15 16 17 18 19 20 21 22 23 24 **25** 26 27 28/29

FEBRUARY

I guess you could call me a neotubist.
It's a bit like the human intestines,
where there's an ambiguity between
the inside and outside, and that
inside/outside dichotomy is blurred,
and that's what I'm interested in.

Toyo Ito

Tod's Omotesando Building, 2003–2004
Toyo Ito & Associates
Tokyo/Japan

1 2 3 4 5 6 7 8 9 10 11 12 13 14 15 16 17 18 19 20 21 22 23 24 25 26 27 28/29

FEBRUARY

Our mind is not free if it is not
the master of its imagination.

Karl Friedrich Schinkel

Château de Châteaudun, stairwell in the Longueville wing, 1170–1491
Châteaudun/France

1 2 3 4 5 6 7 8 9 10 11 12 13 14 15 16 17 18 19 20 21 22 23 24 25 26 **27** 28/29

FEBRUARY

The more we amplify our need and our
possession, the more we involve ourselves in
the blows of fortune and adversity.

Michel de Montaigne

Bally's Hotel, 1981
Las Vegas/USA

1 2 3 4 5 6 7 8 9 10 11 12 13 14 15 16 17 18 19 20 21 22 23 24 25 26 27 28/29

FEBRUARY

You may be able to say in retrospect
that the rule of Bigness – "the
promiscuous proliferation of events in a
single container" – will have applied to
the Bigness that is China.

Rem Koolhaas

Rendering of the China Central Television Headquarters, 2002–2008
Rem Koolhaas, Ole Scheeren
Beijing/China

1 2 3 4 5 6 7 8 9 10 11 12 13 14 15 16 17 18 19 20 21 22 23 24 25 26 27 28 29 30 31

MARCH

People in those old times had
convictions; we moderns only
have opinions. And it needs
more than a mere opinion
to erect a Gothic cathedral.

Heinrich Heine

Cologne Cathedral, façade, 1248–1880
Cologne/Germany

1 2 3 4 5 6 7 8 9 10 11 12 13 14 15 16 17 18 19 20 21 22 23 24 25 26 27 28 29 30 31

MARCH

Even the tallest tower started
from the ground.

Chinese proverb

Jiayuguan Fortress, 1372–1539
Jiayuguan/China

3
1 2 3 4 5 6 7 8 9 10 11 12 13 14 15 16 17 18 19 20 21 22 23 24 25 26 27 28 29 30 31

MARCH

There are seven types of room that are the
most beautiful and well proportioned and
turn out better: they can be made circular,
though these are rare; or square; or their
length will equal the diagonal of the square
of the breadth; or a square and a third;
or a square and a half; or a square and
two-thirds; or two squares.

Andrea Palladio

Hotel Puerta America, guest bedroom, 2003
Zaha Hadid (furniture)
Madrid/Spain

1 2 3 4 5 6 7 8 9 10 11 12 13 14 15 16 17 18 19 20 21 22 23 24 25 26 27 28 29 30 31

MARCH

Symbols are the natural speech of
the soul, a language older and
more universal than words.

C. S. Lewis

Château de Montreuil-Bellay, mid-15th century
Montreuil-Bellay/France

1 2 3 4 5 6 7 8 9 10 11 12 13 14 15 16 17 18 19 20 21 22 23 24 25 26 27 28 29 30 31

MARCH

The wall is the architectural element
that formally represents and makes
visible *enclosed space as such,*
absolutely, as it were, without reference
to secondary concepts.

Gottfried Semper

Apartment façades on the Grand Place in Lille, 17th century
Lille/France

1 2 3 4 5 6 7 8 9 10 11 12 13 14 15 16 17 18 19 20 21 22 23 24 25 26 27 28 29 30 31

MARCH

Architecture is required to do
nothing more than generate "neutral
individuality" for the building and must
not come into conflict with any new
plans for the space that may be
dreamt up in the future.

Léon Wohlhage Wernik Architeken

Indian Embassy, Berlin, 1999–2001
Léon Wohlhage Wernik Architekten
Berlin/Germany

1 2 3 4 5 6 **7** 8 9 10 11 12 13 14 15 16 17 18 19 20 21 22 23 24 25 26 27 28 29 30 31

MARCH

Without Contraries is no progression.
Attraction and Repulsion,
Reason and Energy, Love and Hate,
are necessary to Human existence.

William Blake

Monastery of Saint Miquel de Cuixà, cloister column capital, ca. 1126
Codalet/France

1 2 3 4 5 6 7 8 9 10 11 12 13 14 15 16 17 18 19 20 21 22 23 24 25 26 27 28 29 30 31

MARCH

God makes himself known to the world; He fills up the whole circle of the universe, but makes his particular abode in the center, which is the soul of the just.

Lucian

Padua Cathedral, dome, 1551–1754
Michelangelo Buonarroti et al.
Padua/Italy

1 2 3 4 5 6 7 8 **9** 10 11 12 13 14 15 16 17 18 19 20 21 22 23 24 25 26 27 28 29 30 31

MARCH

Without stirring abroad
One can know the whole world;
Without looking out of the window
One can see the way of heaven.

Lao Tzu

Torre Agbar, façade detail, 2001–2004
Jean Nouvel
Barcelona, Spain

1 2 3 4 5 6 7 8 9 **10** 11 12 13 14 15 16 17 18 19 20 21 22 23 24 25 26 27 28 29 30 31

MARCH

The aspect of the venerable mansion
has always affected me like a human
countenance, bearing the traces not
merely of outward storm and sunshine,
but expressive also, of the long lapse
of mortal life, and accompanying
vicissitudes that have passed within.

Nathaniel Hawthorne

Belvedere Palace (Upper Belvedere), 1721–1723
Johann Lucas von Hildebrandt
Vienna/Austria

1 2 3 4 5 6 7 8 9 10 11 12 13 14 15 16 17 18 19 20 21 22 23 24 25 26 27 28 29 30 31

MARCH

The Renaissance was in my opinion
a retrospective movement;
it was not "rebirth" but decadence.

Auguste Perret

St. Joseph's Church, 1951–1957
Auguste Perret
Le Havre/France

1 2 3 4 5 6 7 8 9 10 11 12 **13** 14 15 16 17 18 19 20 21 22 23 24 25 26 27 28 29 30 31

MARCH

Moderation is a fatal thing.
Nothing succeeds like excess.

Oscar Wilde

Wies Church, view of the north choir, 1745–1754
Johann Baptist and Dominikus Zimmermann
Wies/Germany

1 2 3 4 5 6 7 8 9 10 11 12 13 **14** 15 16 17 18 19 20 21 22 23 24 25 26 27 28 29 30 31

MARCH

For I must tell you that unless you are
resolved to have good and rational
architecture, it is, once again, useless
your thinking about art at all.

William Morris

German Historical Museum, new building, 1998–2004
I. M. Pei
Berlin/Germany

1 2 3 4 5 6 7 8 9 10 11 12 13 14 **15** 16 17 18 19 20 21 22 23 24 25 26 27 28 29 30 31

MARCH

Our life is frittered away by detail…
simplify, simplify.

Henry David Thoreau

Gresham Palace, foyer, 1907
József and Laszló Vágo, Zsigmond Quittner
Budapest/Hungary

1 2 3 4 5 6 7 8 9 10 11 12 13 14 15 **16** 17 18 19 20 21 22 23 24 25 26 27 28 29 30 31

MARCH

Form and color free in us, without any
mediation, like anything else that comes to
consciousness, a particular state of feeling …
the impressions, altogether without associa-
tions … will find an inexhaustible source of
extraordinary and unexpected pleasure.

August Endell

Esplanade Cultural Centre, 2002
DP Architects, Michael Wilford & Partners
Singapore/Singapore

1 2 3 4 5 6 7 8 9 10 11 12 13 14 15 16 17 18 19 20 21 22 23 24 25 26 27 28 29 30 31

MARCH

It is generally allowed that the pleasure
and delight which we feel on the view
of any building, arise from nothing else
but beauty and ornament.

Leon Battista Alberti

Ben Youssef Madrasa in the medina of Marrakech, 14th century
Marrakech/Morocco

1 2 3 4 5 6 7 8 9 10 11 12 13 14 15 16 17 **18** 19 20 21 22 23 24 25 26 27 28 29 30 31

MARCH

When nations grow old, their art grows
complicated and soft. We should try to
return to our youth, to work naively.

Aristide Maillol

The Sage Gateshead (concert hall), 2004
Norman Foster
Gateshead/England

1 2 3 4 5 6 7 8 9 10 11 12 13 14 15 16 17 18 **19** 20 21 22 23 24 25 26 27 28 29 30 31

MARCH

No house should ever be *on* a hill or *on* anything. It should be *of* the hill. Belonging to it. Hill and house should live together each the happier for the other.

Frank Lloyd Wright

Fallingwater, 1935
Frank Lloyd Wright
Mill Run/USA

1 2 3 4 5 6 7 8 9 10 11 12 13 14 15 16 17 18 19 20 21 22 23 24 25 26 27 28 29 30 31

MARCH

In great exploits
our bare attempts suffice.

Erasmus

1 2 3 4 5 6 7 8 9 10 11 12 13 14 15 16 17 18 19 20 21 22 23 24 25 26 27 28 29 30 31

MARCH

I approach each building as a
sculptural object, a spatial container, a
space with light and air, a response to
context and appropriateness of feeling
and spirit.

Frank O. Gehry

Guggenheim Museum Bilbao, 1997
Frank O. Gehry
Bilbao/Spain

1 2 3 4 5 6 7 8 9 10 11 12 13 14 15 16 17 18 19 20 21 22 23 24 25 26 27 28 29 30 31

MARCH

I was glad when they said to me,
"Let us go to the house of the Lord!"

Psalms 122:1

Cathedral of Santiago de Compostela, 1077–1850
Santiago de Campostela/Spain

1 2 3 4 5 6 7 8 9 10 11 12 13 14 15 16 17 18 19 20 21 22 23 24 25 26 27 28 29 30 31

MARCH

Together let us desire, conceive, and create the new structure of the future, which will embrace architecture and sculpture and painting in one unity and which will one day rise toward heaven from the hands of a million workers like the crystal symbol of a new faith.

Walter Gropius

Exhibition building of the Vienna Secession, 1897–1898
Joseph Maria Olbrich
Vienna/Austria

1 2 3 4 5 6 7 8 9 10 11 12 13 14 15 16 17 18 19 20 21 22 23 **24** 25 26 27 28 29 30 31

MARCH

The Pyramid is not important –
I'm sorry to say that. It's a symbol only.
The most important piece of work
in the Louvre is the reorganization
of the entire museum – that is the
important thing, not the Pyramid.

I. M. Pei

Louvre Pyramid, 1985–1989
I. M. Pei
Paris/France

1 2 3 4 5 6 7 8 9 10 11 12 13 14 15 16 17 18 19 20 21 22 23 24 25 26 27 28 29 30 31

MARCH

For fools rush in where
angels fear to tread.

Alexander Pope

Reims Cathedral (Notre-Dame de Reims), west façade, 1212–1300
Reims/France

1 2 3 4 5 6 7 8 9 10 11 12 13 14 15 16 17 18 19 20 21 22 23 24 25 26 27 28 29 30 31

MARCH

It is energy – the central element
of which is will – that produces the
miracles of enthusiasm in all ages.
Everywhere it is the mainspring of what
is called force of character, and the
sustaining power of all great action.

Samuel Smiles

Jewish Museum Berlin, 1992–2001
Daniel Libeskind
Berlin/Germany

1 2 3 4 5 6 7 8 9 10 11 12 13 14 15 16 17 18 19 20 21 22 23 24 25 26 27 28 29 30 31

MARCH

If we wish to understand a nation
by means of its art, let us look at
its architecture or its music.

Oscar Wilde

Semperoper, main entrance, 1871–1878
Gottfried Semper
Dresden/Germany

1 2 3 4 5 6 7 8 9 10 11 12 13 14 15 16 17 18 19 20 21 22 23 24 25 26 27 28 29 30 31

MARCH

Proportion'd like the columns of the temple

Giving and taking strength reciprocal,

And making firm the whole with grace and beauty;

So that no part could be removed without

Infringement of the general symmetry.

Lord Byron

Doge's Palace, 1340–1450
Venice/Italy

1 2 3 4 5 6 7 8 9 10 11 12 13 14 15 16 17 18 19 20 21 22 23 24 25 26 27 28 29 30 31

MARCH

It has the monopoly of space.
Architecture alone of the Arts
can give space its full value.

Geoffrey Scott

Bauhaus building, stairway view, 1925–1926
Walter Gropius
Dessau/Germany

1 2 3 4 5 6 7 8 9 10 11 12 13 14 15 16 17 18 19 20 21 22 23 24 25 26 27 28 29 30 31

MARCH

The Gothic cathedral is a blossoming
in stone subdued by the insatiable
demand of harmony in man.

Ralph Waldo Emerson

Abbey of Cluny, clocktower, 910–1130
Cluny/France

1 2 3 4 5 6 7 8 9 10 11 12 13 14 15 16 17 18 19 20 21 22 23 24 25 26 27 28 29 30 31

MARCH

Color is a power which directly influences the soul. Color is the keyboard, the eyes are the hammer, the soul is the strings.

Wassily Kandinsky

St. Basil Cathedral, 1555–1561
Postnik Yakovlev
Moscow/Russia

1 2 3 4 5 6 7 8 9 10 11 12 13 14 15 16 17 18 19 20 21 22 23 24 25 26 27 28 29 30

APRIL

In matters of art, it is not a question of
asking what previously known useful
things can be brought to the task.
Rather a pure idea of the entire
formation of the work arises
in the soul of the architect.

Karl Friedrich Schinkel

Jagdschloss Granitz (hunting lodge), 1838–1846
Karl Friedrich Schinkel
Rügen/Germany

1 2 3 4 5 6 7 8 9 10 11 12 13 14 15 16 17 18 19 20 21 22 23 24 25 26 27 28 29 30

APRIL

No architecture is so haughty as that
which is simple; which refuses to
address the eye, except in a few clear
and forceful lines; which implies,
in offering so little to our regards,
that all it has offered is perfect.

John Ruskin

Swiss Re-Tower, 2001–2004
Ken Shuttleworth, Norman Foster
London/England

1 2 **3** 4 5 6 7 8 9 10 11 12 13 14 15 16 17 18 19 20 21 22 23 24 25 26 27 28 29 30

APRIL

When I enter a church of the Greeks …
my mind goes to the high honors of our race,
to the glory of our Byzantine tradition.

C. P. Cavafy

Monastery of St. Nicholas Anapausas, 1527
Theophanis Strelitzas (frescoes)
Meteora/Greece

1 2 3 4 5 **6** 7 8 9 10 11 12 13 14 15 16 17 18 19 20 21 22 23 24 25 26 27 28 29 30

APRIL

Art is beauty, the perpetual invention
of detail, the choice of words,
the exquisite care of execution.

Théophile Gautier

Linke Wienzeile 38 apartment building, façade detail, 1898
Otto Wagner
Vienna/Austria

1 2 3 4 5 6 7 8 9 10 11 12 13 14 15 16 17 18 19 20 21 22 23 24 25 26 27 28 29 30

APRIL

The configuration of space begins
with an almost tactile approach to
the world, in an intense, drawn-out,
slow and gradual attaining of objects.

Hotel Puerta America, 10th floor, bedroom, 2003
Arata Isozaki
Madrid/Spain

Arata Isozaki & Asociados España

1 2 3 4 5 6 7 8 9 **10** 11 12 13 14 15 16 17 18 19 20 21 22 23 24 25 26 27 28 29 30

APRIL

The foundation of culture,
as of character, is at last
the moral sentiment.

Ralph Waldo Emerson

Cloister of St. Michel, starting in the 8th century
Saint Donat sur l'Herbasse/France

1 2 3 4 5 6 7 8 9 10 11 12 13 14 15 16 17 18 19 20 21 22 23 24 25 26 27 28 29 30

APRIL

One of the tasks I set for myself was the continuation of the unfinished project of modernism, in the experimental spirit of the early avant-garde – radicalizing some of its compositional techniques like fragmentation and layering.

Zaha Hadid

BMW Plant, Central Building, 2004
Zaha Hadid
Leipzig/Germany

1 2 3 4 5 6 7 8 9 10 11 12 13 14 15 16 17 18 19 20 21 22 23 24 25 26 27 28 29 30

APRIL

According to most architects,
architecture is less the art
of making useful buildings
than that of decorating buildings.

Jean-Nicolas-Louis Durand

St. Peter and St. Paul's Church, 1668–1704
Jan Zaor, Giambattista Frediani
Vilnius/Lithuania

1 2 3 4 5 6 7 8 9 10 11 12 13 14 15 16 17 18 19 20 21 22 23 24 25 26 27 28 29 30

APRIL

The principles discoverable in
the works of the past belong to us;
not so the results. It is taking
the end for the means.

Owen Jones

Zwinger Palace, inner courtyard, 1710–1719
Matthäus Daniel Pöppelmann
Dresden/Germany

1 2 3 4 5 6 7 8 9 10 11 12 13 **14** 15 16 17 18 19 20 21 22 23 24 25 26 27 28 29 30

APRIL

Everything is organic and living,
and therefore the whole world
appears to be a living organism.

Seneca

Einstein Tower, 1919–1922
Erich Mendelssohn
Potsdam/Germany

1 2 3 4 5 6 7 8 9 10 11 12 13 14 **15** 16 17 18 19 20 21 22 23 24 25 26 27 28 29 30

APRIL

I had noted, that all art was then
in truest perfection when it might be
reduced to some natural Principle.
For what are the most judicious
Artisans but the Mimiques of Nature?

Henry Wotton

Maria Luisa Park, Plaza España, 1924–1928
Aníbal González
Seville/Spain

1 2 3 4 5 6 7 8 9 10 11 12 13 14 15 **16** 17 18 19 20 21 22 23 24 25 26 27 28 29 30

APRIL

Nothing requires the architect's
care more than the due proportions
of buildings.

Villa Savoye, view of inner courtyard, 1929–1931
Le Corbusier
Poissy/France

Vitruvius

1 2 3 4 5 6 7 8 9 10 11 12 13 14 15 16 17 18 19 20 21 22 23 24 25 26 27 28 29 30

APRIL

The principle of the Gothic architecture
is infinity made imaginable.

Samuel Taylor Coleridge

Laon Cathedral (Notre-Dame de Laon), crossing, 1170–1235
Laon/France

1 2 3 4 5 6 7 8 9 10 11 12 13 14 15 16 17 **18** 19 20 21 22 23 24 25 26 27 28 29 30

APRIL

In architecture, economy,
far from being, as is often believed,
an obstacle to beauty, is,
on the contrary, its most fertile source.

Jean-Nicolas-Louis Durand

La Vieille Bourse (old mercantile exchange), window detail, 1653
Julien Destrée
Lille/France

1 2 3 4 5 6 7 8 9 10 11 12 13 14 15 16 17 18 **19** 20 21 22 23 24 25 26 27 28 29 30

APRIL

The beauty of a building is based
on its logic and efficiency, not on
ornamentation and the zeitgeist.

Haid Teherani

Hamburg Docklands, 2003–2006
Bothe Richter Teherani
Hamburg/Germany

1 2 3 4 5 6 7 8 9 10 11 12 13 14 15 16 17 18 19 20 21 22 23 24 25 26 27 28 29 30

APRIL

An idea that is developed and put into
action is more important than an idea
that exists only as an idea.

Buddha

Lumbini International Research Institution (LIRI), 1978
Kenzo Tange
Lumbini/Nepal

1 2 3 4 5 6 7 8 9 10 11 12 13 14 15 16 17 18 19 20 21 22 23 24 25 26 27 28 29 30

APRIL

What is eternal is circular and
what is circular is eternal.

Aristotle

Roman theater, 2nd century
Bosra/Syria

1 2 3 4 5 6 7 8 9 10 11 12 13 14 15 16 17 18 19 20 21 22 23 24 25 26 27 28 29 30

APRIL

The architect creates
an autonomous work of art –
for artworks and for people.

Hans Hollein

Museum Abteiberg, façade detail, 1972–1982
Hans Hollein
Mönchengladbach/Germany

1 2 3 4 5 6 7 8 9 10 11 12 13 14 15 16 17 18 19 20 21 22 23 24 25 26 27 28 29 30

APRIL

This the ancients had in view:
we ought to follow their manner,
and observe the kinds of ornaments
used by them, the manner in which
they disposed them to make them
harmonise with the whole.

Giovanni Battista Piranesi

Casa Amatller, roof gable, 1898–1900
Josep Puig i Cadafalch
Barcelona/Spain

1 2 3 4 5 6 7 8 9 10 11 12 13 14 15 16 17 18 19 20 21 22 23 24 25 26 27 28 29 30

APRIL

The high embower'd roof,
With antique pillars, massy proof,
And storied windows, richly dight,
Casting a dim religious light.

John Milton

St. Saveur Church, 15th century
Saorge/France

1 2 3 4 5 6 7 8 9 10 11 12 13 14 15 16 17 18 19 20 21 22 23 24 25 26 27 28 29 30

APRIL

Architecture is not only about
domesticating space, it is also a deep
defence against the terror of time.

Banca Popolare Etica, detail, 2007
Studio Tamassociati
Padua/Italy

Karsten Harries

1 2 3 4 5 6 7 8 9 10 11 12 13 14 15 16 17 18 19 20 21 22 23 24 25 26 27 28 29 30

APRIL

Patience, thou young and
rose-lipp'd cherubin.

William Shakespeare

Cathedral of Syracuse, tympanum of the western portal, 1728
Andrea Palma et al.
Syracuse/Italy

1 2 3 4 5 6 7 8 9 10 11 12 13 14 15 16 17 18 19 20 21 22 23 24 25 26 27 28 29 30

APRIL

Whiteness reflects color, or refracts the
color of nature. It's always changing.
There's enough color all around that
the whiteness enables you really to
perceive color and appreciate it.

Richard Meier

Benedictine Abbey of Neresheim, ceiling vault, 1747–1792
Balthasar Neumann
Neresheim/Germany

1 2 3 4 5 6 7 8 9 10 11 12 13 14 15 16 17 18 19 20 21 22 23 24 25 26 27 28 29 30

APRIL

I think the blurring of the lines between
art and architecture has got to
happen. I don't think these categories
are working very well. I am finding
the crossover much more exhilarating
and much more interesting, and the
collaboration much more interesting.

Frank O. Gehry

DZ Bank, Pariser Platz, atrium, 2001
Frank O. Gehry
Berlin/Germany

1 2 3 4 5 6 7 8 9 10 11 12 13 14 15 16 17 18 19 20 21 22 23 24 25 26 27 28 29 30

APRIL

Such is the city properly styled eternal –
since it is eternal, at least, as regards
the consciousness of the individual.

Henry James

Basilica di Santa Maria del Fiore (Il Duomo), 1296–1436
Florence/Italy

1 2 3 4 5 6 7 8 9 10 11 12 13 14 15 16 17 18 19 20 21 22 23 24 25 26 27 28 29 30 31

MAY

The gospel of elimination is one never preached enough. No matter how much preached, Simplicity is a spiritual ideal seldom organically reached.

Frank Lloyd Wright

Solomon R. Guggenheim Museum, view of the cupola, 1956–1959
Frank Lloyd Wright
New York/USA

1 2 3 4 5 6 7 8 9 10 11 12 13 14 15 16 17 18 19 20 21 22 23 24 25 26 27 28 29 30 31

MAY

A house may be adorned with towers
and battlements … but it should still
maintain the character of a house
of the age and country in which
it is erected.

Richard Payne Knight

Château Azay-le-Rideau, 1518–1527
Azay-le-Rideau/France

1 2 3 4 5 6 7 8 9 10 11 12 13 14 15 16 17 18 19 20 21 22 23 24 25 26 27 28 29 30 31

MAY

It affords me no satisfaction to
commence to spring an arch
before I have got a solid foundation.

Henry David Thoreau

Paris:Sete Store, detail, 1996
Lisbon/Portugal

1 2 3 4 5 6 7 8 9 10 11 12 13 14 15 16 17 18 19 20 21 22 23 24 25 26 27 28 29 30 31

MAY

Beauty will not come at the call of a
legislature … It will come, as always,
unannounced, and spring up between
the feet of brave and earnest men.

Ralph Waldo Emerson

Monticello, ca. 1770
Thomas Jefferson
Charlottesville/USA

1 2 3 4 5 **6** 7 8 9 10 11 12 13 14 15 16 17 18 19 20 21 22 23 24 25 26 27 28 29 30 31

MAY

I consider beauty a basic
requirement of life.

Walter Gropius

Bauhaus building, 1925–1926
Walter Gropius
Dessau/Germany

1 2 3 4 5 6 **7** 8 9 10 11 12 13 14 15 16 17 18 19 20 21 22 23 24 25 26 27 28 29 30 31

MAY

A builder is like a god,
is like a little god.

Renzo Piano

1 2 3 4 5 6 7 **8** 9 10 11 12 13 14 15 16 17 18 19 20 21 22 23 24 25 26 27 28 29 30 31

MAY

They are countless, voiceless,
hopeless as those fallen or fleeing on
Before the high Kings' horses
in the granite of Babylon.

G. K. Chesterton

Ishtar Gate of Nebuchadnezzar's Palace, 575 BCE
Babylon/Iraq

1 2 3 4 5 6 7 8 9 10 11 12 13 14 15 16 17 18 19 20 21 22 23 24 25 26 27 28 29 30 31

MAY

All art constantly aspires towards
the condition of music.

Walter Pater

Opéra Garnier, 1860–1875
Charles Garnier
Paris/France

1 2 3 4 5 6 7 8 9 **10** 11 12 13 14 15 16 17 18 19 20 21 22 23 24 25 26 27 28 29 30 31

MAY

Beauty of style and harmony
and grace and good rhythm
depend on simplicity.

Plato

Glass House, 1947–1949
Philip Johnson
New Canaan/USA

1 2 3 4 5 6 7 8 9 10 11 12 13 14 15 16 17 18 19 20 21 22 23 24 25 26 27 28 29 30 31

MAY

The artist produces for the liberation
of his soul. It is his nature to create
as it is the nature of water
to run down the hill.

W. Somerset Maugham

Pont du Gard, middle of the 1st century CE
Remoulins/France

1 2 3 4 5 6 7 8 9 10 11 12 13 14 15 16 17 18 19 20 21 22 23 24 25 26 27 28 29 30 31

MAY

Modifications in the traditional way
of building are only permitted
if they represent an improvement.

Adolf Loos

Der Neue Zollhof, 1997–1999
Frank O. Gehry
Düsseldorf/Germany

1 2 3 4 5 6 7 8 9 10 11 12 **13** 14 15 16 17 18 19 20 21 22 23 24 25 26 27 28 29 30 31

MAY

Granada is a crown on the forehead
of Spain which they wanted to encrust
with stars. And the Alhambra
(may God protect her!) is a ruby
at the top of that crown.

Ibn Zamrak

Alhambra, Mexuar Palace, façade detail, 2nd half of the 14th century
Granada/Spain

1 2 3 4 5 6 7 8 9 10 11 12 13 14 15 16 17 18 19 20 21 22 23 24 25 26 27 28 29 30 31

MAY

Architecture is a sort of oratory of power by means of forms.

Friedrich Nietzsche

The Great Wall of China at Mutianyu, 6th century
Mutianyu/China

1 2 3 4 5 6 7 8 9 10 11 12 13 14 15 16 17 18 19 20 21 22 23 24 25 26 27 28 29 30 31

MAY

An instinctive taste teaches men
to build their churches in flat countries,
with spire steeples, which, as they
cannot be referred to any other object,
point as with silent finger to the sky
and star.

Samuel Taylor Coleridge

Smolny Convent, Cathedral of the Resurrection, 1749
Bartolomeo Rastrelli
St. Petersburg/Russia

1 2 3 4 5 6 7 8 9 10 11 12 13 14 15 **16** 17 18 19 20 21 22 23 24 25 26 27 28 29 30 31

MAY

Ornaments are in a manner infinite,
and even in small temples there is
always something which we imagine
might or ought to be added.

Leon Battista Alberti

Rouen Cathedral (Notre-Dame de Rouen), detail of the west façade, 1202–1880
Rouen/France

1 2 3 4 5 6 7 8 9 10 11 12 13 14 15 16 17 18 19 20 21 22 23 24 25 26 27 28 29 30 31

MAY

I have always felt that in the plethora
of choices open to an architect,
only self-discipline, the understanding
of physical laws and sympathy
for people's needs and desires
would save him.

Pietro Belluschi

Unité d'habitation, Flatowallee 16, 1956–1958
Le Corbusier
Berlin/Germany

1 2 3 4 5 6 7 8 9 10 11 12 13 14 15 16 17 **18** 19 20 21 22 23 24 25 26 27 28 29 30 31

MAY

We descend by self-exaltation
and ascend by humility.

St. Benedict

St. Joseph's Church, tower, 1951–1957
Auguste Perret
Le Havre/France

1 2 3 4 5 6 7 8 9 10 11 12 13 14 15 16 17 18 **19** 20 21 22 23 24 25 26 27 28 29 30 31

MAY

Architecture is music in space,
as it were a frozen music.

Cité de la Musique, 1986
Bernard Tschumi
Paris/France

Friedrich von Schelling

1 2 3 4 5 6 7 8 9 10 11 12 13 14 15 16 17 18 19 20 21 22 23 24 25 26 27 28 29 30 31

MAY

All that is not perfect down to the
smallest detail is doomed to perish.

Gustav Mahler

Toul Cathedral (Saint-Étienne de Toul), detail, 13th–15th century
Toul/France

1 2 3 4 5 6 7 8 9 10 11 12 13 14 15 16 17 18 19 20 21 22 23 24 25 26 27 28 29 30 31

MAY

They are horrified … at seeing enormous
sums expended in the erection of
buildings whose destination is not
altogether fixed, and which assume
architectural forms whose adaption no
one can perceive. In their view, the
architect is simply an enemy of the
public prosperity.

Eugène-Emmanuel Viollet-le-Duc

Olympic Stadium, 1973–1976
Roger Taillibert
Montreal/Canada

1 2 3 4 5 6 7 8 9 10 11 12 13 14 15 16 17 18 19 20 21 22 23 24 25 26 27 28 29 30 31

MAY

There are but two strong conquerors
of the forgetfulness of men, Poetry
and Architecture; and the latter in
some sort includes the former, and
is mightier in its reality.

John Ruskin

Dilwara Temple, 11th–13th century
Mount Abu/India

1 2 3 4 5 6 7 8 9 10 11 12 13 14 15 16 17 18 19 20 21 22 23 24 25 26 27 28 29 30 31

MAY

Intercultural architecture is a hybrid
architecture, in which elements of
different cultures exist in symbiosis,
an architecture that exists in symbiosis
with the environment through the
symbiosis of tradition and the most
advanced technology.

Kisho Kurokawa

The National Art Center, Tokyo (Roppongi), 2000–2006
Kisho Kurokawa
Tokyo/Japan

1 2 3 4 5 6 7 8 9 10 11 12 13 14 15 16 17 18 19 20 21 22 23 24 25 26 27 28 29 30 31

MAY

Those who look for the laws of Nature
as a support for their new works
collaborate with the creator.

Antoni Gaudí

1 2 3 4 5 6 7 8 9 10 11 12 13 14 15 16 17 18 19 20 21 22 23 24 25 26 27 28 29 30 31

MAY

A Poet a Painter a Musician an
Architect: the Man or Woman who is
not one of these is not a Christian.

William Blake

Notre-Dame de la Garde, ceiling mosaics, 1853–1864
Henri-Jacques Espérandieu
Marseilles, France

1 2 3 4 5 6 7 8 9 10 11 12 13 14 15 16 17 18 19 20 21 22 23 24 25 26 27 28 29 30 31

MAY

No person who is not a great sculptor
or painter can be an architect.
If he is not a sculptor or painter,
he can only be a builder.

John Ruskin

British Embassy, Berlin, 1998–2000
Michael Wilford & Partners
Berlin/Germany

1 2 3 4 5 6 7 8 9 10 11 12 13 14 15 16 17 18 19 20 21 22 23 24 25 26 27 28 29 30 31

MAY

There is no art more akin to mysticism
than architecture.

Alexander Herzen

Dai Miao Temple Complex, detail, ca. 1000 BCE
Tai'an/China

1 2 3 4 5 6 7 8 9 10 11 12 13 14 15 16 17 18 19 20 21 22 23 24 25 26 27 28 29 30 31

MAY

Nothing shall be to come,
and nothing past,
But an eternal now shall ever last.
Though time shall be no more,
yet space shall give
A nobler theatre to love and live.

Petrarch

Casa della Caccia antica, mosaic, 1st century BCE
Pompeii/Italy

1 2 3 4 5 6 7 8 9 10 11 12 13 14 15 16 17 18 19 20 21 22 23 24 25 26 27 28 29 30 31

MAY

You are weary at last of this ancient world
Shepherdess, O Eiffel Tower, your flock
of bridges is bleating this morning.
You have lived long enough with
Greek and Roman antiquity.

Guillaume Apollinaire

1 2 3 4 5 6 7 8 9 10 11 12 13 14 15 16 17 18 19 20 21 22 23 24 25 26 27 28 29 30 31

MAY

The moment of truth, the composition of elements, the selection of forms, scale, materials, color, finally, all the same issues facing the painter and the sculptor. Architecture is surely an art.

Frank O. Gehry

Walt Disney Concert Hall, façade detail, 2003
Frank O. Gehry
Los Angeles/USA

1 2 3 4 5 6 7 8 9 10 11 12 13 14 15 16 17 18 19 20 21 22 23 24 25 26 27 28 29 30 31

MAY

I often come and walk here to restore
to my soul that serenity which it
sometimes loses: the sight of such
a monument is like continual and
sustained music, which waits to do
you good when you approach.

Madame de Staël

Basilica of St. Peter, cupola, 1547
Michelangelo Buonarroti
Rome/Italy

1 2 3 4 5 6 7 8 9 10 11 12 13 14 15 16 17 18 19 20 21 22 23 24 25 26 27 28 29 30

JUNE

Tell me … have you not noticed, in
walking about this city, that among
the buildings with which it is peopled,
certain are mute; others speak;
and others, finally – and they are
the most rare – sing?

Paul Valéry

Casa da Música, 2005
Rem Koolhaas
Oporto/Portugal

1 2 3 4 5 6 7 8 9 10 11 12 13 14 15 16 17 18 19 20 21 22 23 24 25 26 27 28 29 30

JUNE

The two great rules for design are these:
first, that there should be no features about
a building which are not necessary for
convenience, construction or propriety;
second, that all ornament should consist
of enrichment of the essential construction
of the building.

Augustus Pugin

Westminster Palace, 1834–1860
Charles Barry and Augustus Pugin
London/England

1 2 **3** 4 5 6 7 8 9 10 11 12 13 14 15 16 17 18 19 20 21 22 23 24 25 26 27 28 29 30

JUNE

In paring down architecture to its
barest yet most sumptuous essentials,
he has reaffirmed architecture's
indispensable place in a fragile world.

Thermal Baths Vals, 1996
Peter Zumthor
Vals/Switzerland

Pritzker Architecture Prize Jury Citation

1 2 3 4 5 6 7 8 9 10 11 12 13 14 15 16 17 18 19 20 21 22 23 24 25 26 27 28 29 30

JUNE

Gentility and synagogue,
in sweet metric voices,
one of you acclaims God,
the other celebrates a man.

Sor Juana Ines de la Cruz

Church of Santa Prisca, 1751–1758
Taxco/Mexico

1 2 3 4 **5** 6 7 8 9 10 11 12 13 14 15 16 17 18 19 20 21 22 23 24 25 26 27 28 29 30

JUNE

If one may build upon a river,
it will be both convenient and beautiful.

Château de Chenonceau, 1515–1522
Chenonceau/France

Andrea Palladio

1 2 3 4 5 6 7 8 9 10 11 12 13 14 15 16 17 18 19 20 21 22 23 24 25 26 27 28 29 30

JUNE

The very same numbers that cause
sounds to have that *concinnitas*
(harmony) pleasing to the ears,
can also fill the eyes and mind
with wondrous delight.

Leon Battista Alberti

Basilica di Santa Maria del Fiore (Il Duomo), west and south façades, 1296–1436
Florence/Italy

1 2 3 4 5 6 7 8 9 10 11 12 13 14 15 16 17 18 19 20 21 22 23 24 25 26 27 28 29 30

JUNE

To those whose talents are above
mediocrity, the highest subjects
may be announced.

Confucius

Jin Mao Tower, 1994–1998
Skidmore, Owings & Merrill LLP (SOM)
Shanghai/China

1 2 3 4 5 6 7 8 9 **10** 11 12 13 14 15 16 17 18 19 20 21 22 23 24 25 26 27 28 29 30

JUNE

I never weary of great churches. It is my
favorite kind of mountain scenery.
Mankind was never so happily inspired
as when it made a cathedral.

The Cathedral of Siena (Santa Maria Assunta), façade, 1215–1263
Siena/Italy

Robert Louis Stevenson

1 2 3 4 5 6 7 8 9 10 11 12 13 14 15 16 17 18 19 20 21 22 23 24 25 26 27 28 29 30

JUNE

He must not demolish, but build.
He must raise temples where
mankind may come and partake
of the purest pleasure.

Johann Wolfgang von Goethe

New Yorker Skyline with rendering of the Freedom Towers, 2004–?
Daniel Libeskind
New York/USA

1 2 3 4 5 6 7 8 9 10 11 12 13 14 15 16 17 18 19 20 21 22 23 24 25 26 27 28 29 30

JUNE

On painted ceilings you devoutly stare,
Where sprawl the saints of
    Verrio or Laguerre,
On gilded clouds in fair expansion lie,
And bring all Paradise before your eye.

Alexander Pope

Burghley House, 1556–1587
William Cecil (Lord Burghley)
Stamford/England

1 2 3 4 5 6 7 8 9 10 11 12 **13** 14 15 16 17 18 19 20 21 22 23 24 25 26 27 28 29 30

JUNE

There is a powerful need for symbolism,
and that means the architecture
must have something that appeals
to the human heart.

Kenzo Tange

Rendering of the Freedom Tower (replacement of the Twin Towers), 2003
Skidmore Owings & Merrill LLP (SOM)
New York/USA

1 2 3 4 5 6 7 8 9 10 11 12 13 14 15 16 17 18 19 20 21 22 23 24 25 26 27 28 29 30

JUNE

God is in the Details.

Ludwig Mies van der Rohe

Konark Sun Temple, wheel of the Sun Chariot, mid-13th century
Konark/India

1 2 3 4 5 6 7 8 9 10 11 12 13 14 15 16 17 18 19 20 21 22 23 24 25 26 27 28 29 30

JUNE

The place is nicely situated and one of the loveliest and most charming that one could hope to find; for it lies on the slopes of a hill, which is very easy to reach…. Because one takes pleasure in the beautiful view on all four sides, loggias were built on all four façades.

Andrea Palladio

Villa La Rotonda, from 1566
Andrea Palladio
Vicenza/Italy

1 2 3 4 5 6 7 8 9 10 11 12 13 14 15 16 17 18 19 20 21 22 23 24 25 26 27 28 29 30

JUNE

Harmony is an obscure and
difficult musical science.

Vitruvius

Auditorium of Tenerife, hall, 1989–2003
Santiago Calatrava
Santa Cruz/Spain

1 2 3 4 5 6 7 8 9 10 11 12 13 14 15 16 17 **18** 19 20 21 22 23 24 25 26 27 28 29 30

JUNE

Wherever there is craftsmanship
there is art.

Alberto Moravia

Casa Malaparte, 1938–1943
Adalberto Libera
Capri/Italy

1 2 3 4 5 6 7 8 9 10 11 12 13 14 15 16 17 18 19 20 21 22 23 24 25 26 27 28 29 30

JUNE

In mighty enterprises, it is enough to
have had the determination.

Sextus Propertius

US Capitol Building, 1792–1909
Washington, DC/USA

1 2 3 4 5 6 7 8 9 10 11 12 13 14 15 16 17 18 19 20 21 22 23 24 25 26 27 28 29 30

JUNE

I take it as self-evident that a building,
quite devoid of ornament, may convey
a noble and dignified sentiment by
virtue of mass and proportion.

Louis Sullivan

National Congress of Brazil, 1956
Oscar Niemeyer
Brasilia/Brazil

1 2 3 4 5 6 7 8 9 10 11 12 13 14 15 16 17 18 19 20 21 22 23 24 25 26 27 28 29 30

JUNE

Without optimism I couldn't build
anything. And I hope my architecture
is also architecture of optimism.

Cupola of the Reichstag, 1994–1999
Norman Foster
Berlin/Germany

Norman Foster

1 2 3 4 5 6 7 8 9 10 11 12 13 14 15 16 17 18 19 20 21 22 23 24 25 26 27 28 29 30

JUNE

There is a very holy and a very terrible
isolation for the conscience of every
man who seeks to read the destiny in
affairs for others as well as for himself,
for a nation as well as for individuals.

Woodrow Wilson

Lincoln Memorial, 1915
Henry Bacon
Washington, DC/USA

1 2 3 4 5 6 7 8 9 10 11 12 13 14 15 16 17 18 19 20 21 22 23 24 25 26 27 28 29 30

JUNE

Nature is a temple of living pillars

Where often words emerge, confused and dim;

And man goes through this forest,

with familiar eyes of symbols

always watching him.

Charles Baudelaire

Priory of Santa María de Serrabona, after 1082
Boule-d'Amont/France

1 2 3 4 5 6 7 8 9 10 11 12 13 14 15 16 17 18 19 20 21 22 23 24 25 26 27 28 29 30

JUNE

Nearly everything that encloses space
on a scale sufficient for a human
being to move in is a building;
the term architecture applies only
to buildings designed with a view
to aesthetic appeal.

Nikolaus Pevsner

Allianz Arena, 2002–2005
Herzog & de Meuron
Munich/Germany

1 2 3 4 5 6 7 8 9 10 11 12 13 14 15 16 17 18 19 20 21 22 23 24 25 26 27 28 29 30

JUNE

If cities were built by the sound of music, then some edifices would appear to be constructed by grave, solemn tones, – others to have danced forth to light fantastic airs.

Nathaniel Hawthorne

Opera, with the courtyard of the Lyon city hall in the foreground, 1993
Jean Nouvel
Lyon/France

1 2 3 4 5 6 7 8 9 10 11 12 13 14 15 16 17 18 19 20 21 22 23 24 25 26 27 28 29 30

JUNE

The most powerful men have always
inspired the architects; the architect
has always been influenced by power.

Friedrich Nietzsche

Palace of Versailles, royal chapel, 1689–1708
Jules Hardouin-Mansart
Versailles/France

1 2 3 4 5 6 7 8 9 10 11 12 13 14 15 16 17 18 19 20 21 22 23 24 25 26 27 28 29 30

JUNE

The world is three days:
As for yesterday, it has vanished,
along with all that was in it.
As for tomorrow, you may never see it.
As for today, it is yours, so work in it.

Hassan al-Basri

Museum of Islamic Art, 2008
I. M. Pei
Doha/Qatar

1 2 3 4 5 6 7 8 9 10 11 12 13 14 15 16 17 18 19 20 21 22 23 24 25 26 27 28 29 30

JUNE

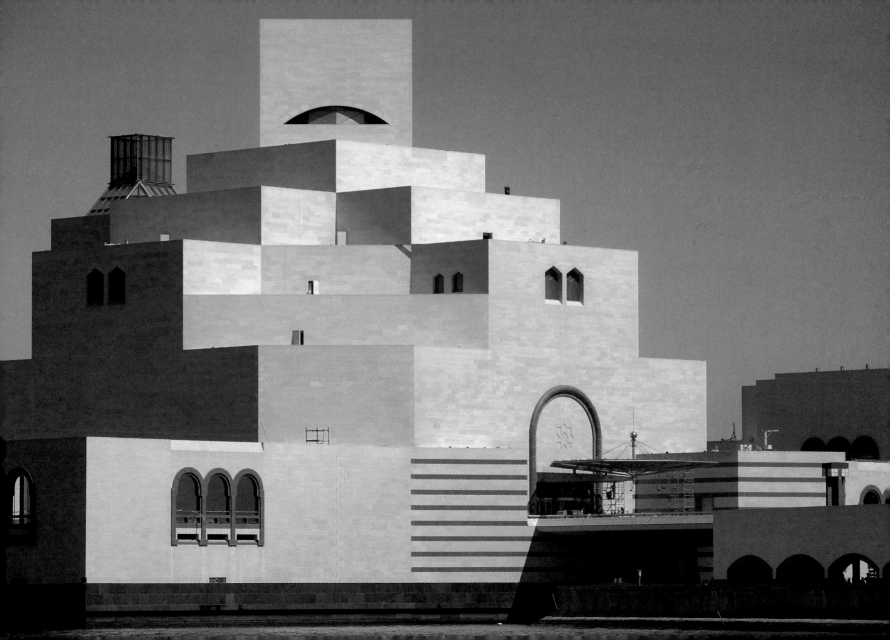

Style is a fraud. I always felt the Greeks
were hiding behind their columns.

Willem De Kooning

Erechtheum, Acropolis, 420–406 BCE
Philocles, Archilochos
Athens/Greece

1 2 3 4 5 6 7 8 9 10 11 12 13 14 15 16 17 18 19 20 21 22 23 24 25 26 27 28 29 30

JUNE

Harrow the house of the dead;
look shining at New styles of
architecture, a change of heart.

W. H. Auden

Tate Gallery of Modern Art, 1947–1963/2000
Giles Gilbert Scott, Herzog & de Meuron
London/England

1 2 3 4 5 6 7 8 9 10 11 12 13 14 15 16 17 18 19 20 21 22 23 24 25 26 27 28 29 30

JUNE

An aesthetic based on human
emotions does not become outdated
even with the perennial changing
of fashions in literature and in art.

Gao Xingjian

Church of St. Charalambos, Agios Stephanos Monastery, 14th century
Meteora/Greece

1 2 3 4 5 6 7 8 9 10 11 12 13 14 15 16 17 18 19 20 21 22 23 24 25 26 27 28 29 30 31

JULY

You create it in its loveliness,
and leave it, as her Maker left Eve.
Not unadorned, I believe,
but so well adorned as to need
no feather crowns.

John Ruskin

Doge's Palace, façade detail, after 1340
Venice/Italy

The artistic taste of the Catholic priests
is appalling and I am most anxious
to have a Catholic church in which
everything is genuine and good,
and not tawdry and ostentatious.

Giles Gilbert Scott

Dio Padre Misericordioso (Jubilee Church), 2003
Richard Meier
Rome/Italy

1 2 3 4 5 6 7 8 9 10 11 12 13 14 15 16 17 18 19 20 21 22 23 24 25 26 27 28 29 30 31

JULY

This made of the church for me something
entirely different from the rest of the town –
an edifice occupying, so to speak,
a four-dimensional space – the name of
the fourth being Time.

Marcel Proust

Amiens Cathedral (Notre-Dame d'Amiens), northern transept, after 1218
Robert de Luzarches
Amiens/France

1 2 3 4 **5** 6 7 8 9 10 11 12 13 14 15 16 17 18 19 20 21 22 23 24 25 26 27 28 29 30 31

JULY

America does not repel the past or
what it has produced under its forms
or amid other politics or the idea
of castes or the old religions.

Walt Whitman

US Capitol Building, cupola, 1793–1863
Washington, DC/USA

1 2 3 4 5 **6** 7 8 9 10 11 12 13 14 15 16 17 18 19 20 21 22 23 24 25 26 27 28 29 30 31

JULY

Add a sprinkling of folly
to your long deliberations.

Horace

Church of Santa Chiara, 18th century
Rosario Gagliardi
Noto/Italy

1 2 3 4 5 6 7 8 9 10 11 12 13 14 15 16 17 18 19 20 21 22 23 24 25 26 27 28 29 30 31

JULY

Architecture is the art which so
disposes and adorns the edifices
raised by man, for whatsoever uses,
that the sight of them may
contribute to his mental health,
power, and pleasure.

John Ruskin

Palace of Versailles, Hall of Mirrors, 1678
Versailles/France

1 2 3 4 5 6 7 8 9 10 11 12 13 14 15 16 17 18 19 20 21 22 23 24 25 26 27 28 29 30 31

JULY

As an architect, you design for the
present, with an awareness of the past,
for a future which is essentially unknown.

Norman Foster

Smithsonian American Art Museum, Kogod Courtyard, 2007
Norman Foster
Washington, DC/USA

1 2 3 4 5 6 7 8 9 10 11 12 13 14 15 16 17 18 19 20 21 22 23 24 25 26 27 28 29 30 31

JULY

You employ stone, wood and
concrete, and with these materials
you build houses and palaces:
that is construction. Ingenuity is at work.
But suddenly you touch my heart,
you do me good. I am happy and I say:
"This is beautiful. That is architecture."

Le Corbusier

Villa Savoye, exterior view, 1929–1931
Le Corbusier
Poissy/France

1 2 3 4 5 6 7 8 9 10 11 12 13 14 15 16 17 18 19 20 21 22 23 24 25 26 27 28 29 30 31

JULY

O fair foundation laid whereon to build
Their ruin!

John Milton

Erechtheum, Caryatides, 406 BCE
Philocles, Archilochos
Athens/Greece

1 2 3 4 5 6 7 8 9 10 11 12 13 14 15 16 17 18 19 20 21 22 23 24 25 26 27 28 29 30 31

JULY

Do not treat your marble as if it was ordinary stone and build a house of mere blocks of it. For it is indeed a precious stone, this marble of yours, and only workmen of nobility of invention and delicacy of hand should be allowed to touch it at all, carving it into noble statues or into beautiful decoration.

Oscar Wilde

Basilica di San Lorenzo, Medici capital, view of the cupola, 1520–1534
Michelangelo Buonarroti
Florence/Italy

1 2 3 4 5 6 7 8 9 10 11 12 **13** 14 15 16 17 18 19 20 21 22 23 24 25 26 27 28 29 30 31

JULY

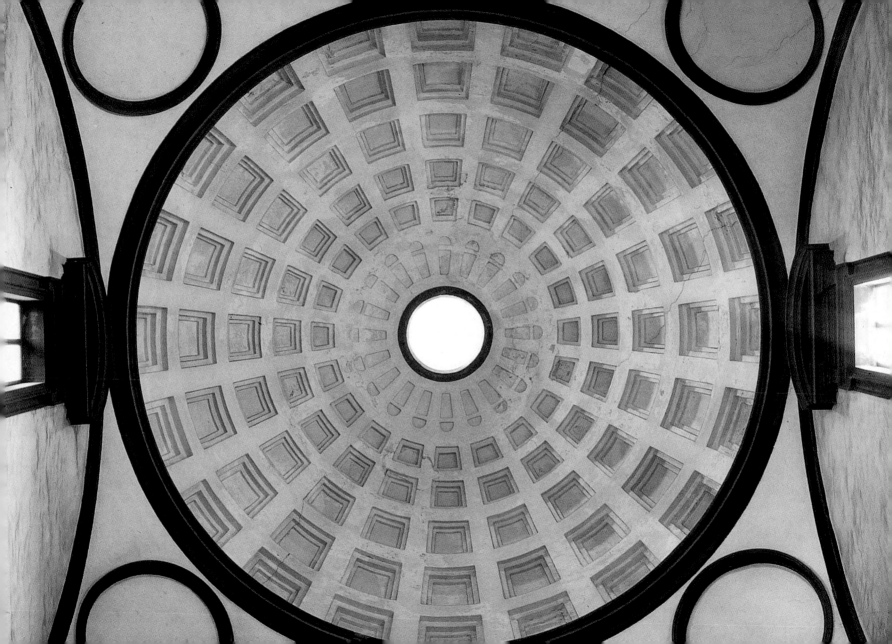

That which I was seeing seemed to me
a smile of the Universe.

Dante Alighieri

Wat Arun, detail, 17th century
Bangkok/Thailand

1 2 3 4 5 6 7 8 9 10 11 12 13 **14** 15 16 17 18 19 20 21 22 23 24 25 26 27 28 29 30 31

JULY

A walk of trees is more beautiful than the most artificial portico; but these not being easily preserved in market-places, they made the more durable shades of porticoes.

Christopher Wren

Alhambra, Palace of Charles V, portico, 1528
Pedro Machuca
Granada/Spain

1 2 3 4 5 6 7 8 9 10 11 12 13 14 **15** 16 17 18 19 20 21 22 23 24 25 26 27 28 29 30 31

JULY

When we build let us think
we build forever.

John Ruskin

Dome of the Rock, 7th–8th century CE
Jerusalem/Israel

1 2 3 4 5 6 7 8 9 10 11 12 13 14 15 **16** 17 18 19 20 21 22 23 24 25 26 27 28 29 30 31

JULY

Harmony would lose its attractiveness
if it did not have a background
of discord.

Chinese proverb

Olympic Stadium Munich, roof structure, 1968–1972
Günther Behnisch
Munich/Germany

1 2 3 4 5 6 7 8 9 10 11 12 13 14 15 16 17 18 19 20 21 22 23 24 25 26 27 28 29 30 31

JULY

For me, right from the beginning the "art" of architecture has always been the priority. That's what I trained to do.

James Stirling

Neue Staatsgalerie Stuttgart, 1979–1984
James Stirling
Stuttgart/Germany

1 2 3 4 5 6 7 8 9 10 11 12 13 14 15 16 17 18 **19** 20 21 22 23 24 25 26 27 28 29 30 31

JULY

Architecture is the great book
of humanity, the principal expression
of man in his different stages
of development, either as a force
or as an intelligence.

Victor Hugo

Notre-Dame de Paris, west façade, 1163–1345
Paris/France

1 2 3 4 5 6 7 8 9 10 11 12 13 14 15 16 17 18 19 20 21 22 23 24 25 26 27 28 29 30 31

JULY

Nature does not complete things.
She is chaotic. Man must finish,
and he does so by making a garden
and building a wall.

Robert Frost

Villa Garzoni, garden, since 1652
Collodi/Italy

1 2 3 4 5 6 7 8 9 10 11 12 13 14 15 16 17 18 19 20 21 22 23 24 25 26 27 28 29 30 31

JULY

I dreamed That stone by stone I reared

a sacred fane,

A temple, neither Pagoda,

Mosque nor Church,

But loftier, simpler, always open-doored

To every breath from heaven,

and Truth and Peace

And Love and Justice came and dwelt therein.

Alfred Lord Tennyson

Abbey of Thoronet, 1160–1180
Le Thoronet/France

22

1 2 3 4 5 6 7 8 9 10 11 12 13 14 15 16 17 18 19 20 21 22 23 24 25 26 27 28 29 30 31

JULY

For all life is a dream, and dreams
themselves are only dreams.

Pedro Calderón de la Barca

Mezquita of Cordoba, ceiling detail, 600–987
Cordoba/Spain

1 2 3 4 5 6 7 8 9 10 11 12 13 14 15 16 17 18 19 20 21 22 **23** 24 25 26 27 28 29 30 31

JULY

To know what to leave out and what to
put in, just where and just how –
Ah, *that* is to have been educated
in knowledge of SIMPLICITY.

Frank Lloyd Wright

Auditorium Parco della Musica, 1994–2002
Renzo Piano
Rome/Italy

1 2 3 4 5 6 7 8 9 10 11 12 13 14 15 16 17 18 19 20 21 22 23 **24** 25 26 27 28 29 30 31

JULY

You will also find that God is a number,
an intelligence, a harmony.

Lucian

1 2 3 4 5 6 7 8 9 10 11 12 13 14 15 16 17 18 19 20 21 22 23 24 25 26 27 28 29 30 31

JULY

It is in vain to expect any great progress in the
sciences by the superinducing or engrafting
new matters upon old. An instauration must be
made from the very foundations, if we do not
wish to revolve forever in a circle, making only
some slight and contemptible progress.

Sir Francis Bacon

Atomium, 1958
André Waterkeyn
Brussels/Belgium

1 2 3 4 5 6 7 8 9 10 11 12 13 14 15 16 17 18 19 20 21 22 23 24 25 26 27 28 29 30 31

JULY

Sculpture is more divine,
and more like Nature,
That fashions all her works in high relief,
And that is Sculpture.

Henry Wadsworth Longfellow

Temple of Isis on Agilika Island, eastern colonnade, 380–145 BCE
Agilika/Egypt

1 2 3 4 5 6 7 8 9 10 11 12 13 14 15 16 17 18 19 20 21 22 23 24 25 26 27 28 29 30 31

JULY

Building a structure like that,
you risk falling into the picaresque.
But you have to run some risks –
it's part of the profession.

Renzo Piano

Centre Culturel Tjibaou, 1991–1998
Renzo Piano
Noumea/New Caledonia

1 2 3 4 5 6 7 8 9 10 11 12 13 14 15 16 17 18 19 20 21 22 23 24 25 26 27 28 29 30 31

JULY

Architecture aims at eternity;
and therefore the only Thing
uncapable of Modes and Fashions
in its Principals, the *Orders*.

Christopher Wren

St. Paul's Cathedral, façade, 1677–1708
Christopher Wren
London/England

1 2 3 4 5 6 7 8 9 10 11 12 13 14 15 16 17 18 19 20 21 22 23 24 25 26 27 28 29 30 31

JULY

No single thing abides; but all things flow.

Fragment to fragment clings –

the things thus grow

Until we know them and name them.

By degrees

They melt, are no more the things we know.

Lucretius

Ruins of ancient Palmyra, 1st–2nd century CE
Palmyra/Syria

1 2 3 4 5 6 7 8 9 10 11 12 13 14 15 16 17 18 19 20 21 22 23 24 25 26 27 28 29 30 31

JULY

It's the answer to a question you might
never ask, which is: "If you have an
infinite array of soap bubbles of equal
volume, what shape are they?"
In other words, what is the most efficient
way of dividing space with structure?

Tristram Carfrae

National Aquatics Center ("Water Cube"), 2003–2007
PTW, Arup
Beijing/China

1 2 3 4 5 6 7 8 9 10 11 12 13 14 15 16 17 18 19 20 21 22 23 24 25 26 27 28 29 30 31

JULY

They say that this light,
proceeding from the top,
was the emblem of that God who
was superior to all the other deities....
It seems, in effect, that this language
is more fitting than speech to religion.

Madame de Staël

Pantheon, interior view of the cupola, 110 CE
Rome/Italy

1 2 3 4 5 6 7 8 9 10 11 12 13 14 15 16 17 18 19 20 21 22 23 24 25 26 27 28 29 30 31

AUGUST

I have found a paper of mine among some others in which I call architecture "petrified music." Really there is something in this; the tone of mind produced by architecture approaches the effect of music.

Johann Wolfgang von Goethe

Sydney Opera House, 1959–1973
Jørn Oberg Utzon
Sydney/Australia

1 2 3 4 5 6 7 8 9 10 11 12 13 14 15 16 17 18 19 20 21 22 23 24 25 26 27 28 29 30 31

AUGUST

A thousand years their cloudy wings expand
Around me, and a dying Glory smiles
O'er the far times, when many a subject land
Look'd to the winged Lion's marble pines,
Where Venice sate in state,
throned on her hundred isles.

Lord Byron

Bridge of Sighs, 1600–1603
Antonio Contino
Venice/Italy

1 2 3 4 5 6 7 8 9 10 11 12 13 14 15 16 17 18 19 20 21 22 23 24 25 26 27 28 29 30 31

AUGUST

Ornamentation is the principal part
of architecture.

John Ruskin

Munich Residence, ballroom, 1825–1842
Leo von Klenze
Munich/Germany

1 2 3 4 5 6 7 8 9 10 11 12 13 14 15 16 17 18 19 20 21 22 23 24 25 26 27 28 29 30 31

AUGUST

Things are pretty, graceful, rich,
elegant, handsome, but,
until they speak to the imagination,
not yet beautiful.

Ralph Waldo Emerson

Louvre Pyramid, interior view, 1985–1989
I. M. Pei
Paris/France

1 2 3 4 5 **6** 7 8 9 10 11 12 13 14 15 16 17 18 19 20 21 22 23 24 25 26 27 28 29 30 31

AUGUST

I, for my part, hate everything
that favors of luxury or profusion,
and am best pleased with those
ornaments which arise principally
from the ingenuity and beauty
of the contrivance.

Leon Battista Alberti

Chrysler Building, façade ornament, 1928–1930
William van Alen
New York/USA

1 2 3 4 5 6 7 8 9 10 11 12 13 14 15 16 17 18 19 20 21 22 23 24 25 26 27 28 29 30 31

AUGUST

Men had not a hammer to begin with,
not a syllabled articulation: they had it
all to make; and they have made it.

Thomas Carlyle

La Grande Arche, 1984–1989
Johann Otto von Spreckelsen and Paul Andreu
Paris/France

1 2 3 4 5 6 7 **8** 9 10 11 12 13 14 15 16 17 18 19 20 21 22 23 24 25 26 27 28 29 30 31

AUGUST

The truth, even if hundreds of years old,
has more spiritual connection with us
than the lie which strides beside us.

Adolf Loos

Medina Azahara, detail, 936–976
Cordoba/Spain

1 2 3 4 5 6 7 8 9 10 11 12 13 14 15 16 17 18 19 20 21 22 23 24 25 26 27 28 29 30 31

AUGUST

Only when the form is clear to you
will the spirit become clear too.

Robert Schumann

L'Hôtel de Cluny, gable, 1485–1490
Paris/France

1 2 3 4 5 6 7 8 9 **10** 11 12 13 14 15 16 17 18 19 20 21 22 23 24 25 26 27 28 29 30 31

AUGUST

The sole path to modern greatness
lay in the study of the ancient.

Johann Joachim Winckelmann

Altes Museum, rotunda, 1825–1828
Karl Friedrich Schinkel
Berlin/Germany

1 2 3 4 5 6 7 8 9 10 11 12 13 14 15 16 17 18 19 20 21 22 23 24 25 26 27 28 29 30 31

AUGUST

Beauty will derive from a graceful
shape and the relationship of the
whole to the parts, and of the parts
among themselves and to the whole,
because buildings must appear to be
like complete and well-defined bodies.

Andrea Palladio

Solomon R. Guggenheim Museum, 1956–1959
Frank Lloyd Wright
New York/USA

1 2 3 4 5 6 7 8 9 10 11 12 13 14 15 16 17 18 19 20 21 22 23 24 25 26 27 28 29 30 31

AUGUST

Forms are the very food of faith.

John Henry Newman

1 2 3 4 5 6 7 8 9 10 11 12 **13** 14 15 16 17 18 19 20 21 22 23 24 25 26 27 28 29 30 31

AUGUST

Artistic expression is a manifestation
of the unity of design and material.

German Pavilion for the International Exhibition, 1929
Ludwig Mies van der Rohe
Barcelona/Spain

Ludwig Mies van der Rohe

1 2 3 4 5 6 7 8 9 10 11 12 13 14 15 16 17 18 19 20 21 22 23 24 25 26 27 28 29 30 31

AUGUST

For construction, do not the branches
of the trees, the stems, by turn rigid and
undulating, furnish us with models?

Hector Germain Guimard

Medina Azahara, column capital, 936–945
Cordoba/Spain

1 2 3 4 5 6 7 8 9 10 11 12 13 14 **15** 16 17 18 19 20 21 22 23 24 25 26 27 28 29 30 31

AUGUST

Let the beauty of what you love
be what you do.

Jalal ad-Din Umi

Kabir Jaame Mosque, 10th–11th century
Yazd/Iran

1 2 3 4 5 6 7 8 9 10 11 12 13 14 15 **16** 17 18 19 20 21 22 23 24 25 26 27 28 29 30 31

AUGUST

Bridges represent archetypal problems.
They are artifacts that bring you across or
around an obstacle. So they have an
unbelievable force. It's a very pure and
almost existential need – to go across
something in order to leave or to arrive,
to have access to other places.

Santiago Calatrava

Golden Jubilee Bridges, 2002
Lifschutz Davidson
London/England

1 2 3 4 5 6 7 8 9 10 11 12 13 14 15 16 **17** 18 19 20 21 22 23 24 25 26 27 28 29 30 31

AUGUST

If the goal of earlier monumental architecture was to make Beauty predominate over utility, it is undeniable that in the mechanical order the dominant aim is *utility, strictly utility.*

Fernand Léger

Villa Savoye, interior spiral staircase, 1929–1931
Le Corbusier
Poissy/France

1 2 3 4 5 6 7 8 9 10 11 12 13 14 15 16 17 18 19 20 21 22 23 24 25 26 27 28 29 30 31

AUGUST

A rock pile ceases to be a rock pile
the moment a single man
contemplates it, bearing within him
the image of a cathedral.

Antoine de Saint Exupéry

Angkor Wat temple complex, 12th century
Angkor Wat/Cambodia

1 2 3 4 5 6 7 8 9 10 11 12 13 14 15 16 17 18 19 20 21 22 23 24 25 26 27 28 29 30 31

AUGUST

The design of a temple depends on
symmetry, the principles of which must
be most carefully observed by the
architect. They are due to proportion,
what the Greeks call *analogia*.

Vitruvius

Maison Carré, ca. 19 BCE
Nîmes/France

1 2 3 4 5 6 7 8 9 10 11 12 13 14 15 16 17 18 19 20 21 22 23 24 25 26 27 28 29 30 31

AUGUST

Architecture should be a sort of media-
clothing, which is necessary in order for
man to have a relationship with and
integrate himself into the environment.

Toyo Ito

Mikimoto Building, façade detail, 2005
Toyo Ito
Tokyo/Japan

1 2 3 4 5 6 7 8 9 10 11 12 13 14 15 16 17 18 19 20 21 22 23 24 25 26 27 28 29 30 31

AUGUST

Our civilized world, then,
is only a great masquerade.

Arthur Schopenhauer

Palace in Xlapak, detail of the middle mosaic mask, 10th century
Yucatan/Mexico

1 2 3 4 5 6 7 8 9 10 11 12 13 14 15 16 17 18 19 20 21 22 23 24 25 26 27 28 29 30 31

AUGUST

Form is everything.

Oscar Wilde

Château de Blois, spiral staircase, François I Renaissance wing, 16th century
Blois/France

1 2 3 4 5 6 7 8 9 10 11 12 13 14 15 16 17 18 19 20 21 22 23 24 25 26 27 28 29 30 31

AUGUST

In preparing a design, Tange arrives at
shapes that lift our hearts because
they seem to emerge from some
ancient and dimly remembered past
and yet are breathtakingly of today.

Pritzker Architecture Prize Jury Citation

Museum of Asian Art, 1987–1988
Kenzo Tange
Nice/France

1 2 3 4 5 6 7 8 9 10 11 12 13 14 15 16 17 18 19 20 21 22 23 24 25 26 27 28 29 30 31

AUGUST

When the Moors withdrew from
Andalusia they left their architecture
behind them, and a great many
of their customs.

Stendhal

Alcázar of Seville, Ambassadors' Hall, dome ceiling, 1427
Seville/Spain

1 2 3 4 5 6 7 8 9 10 11 12 13 14 15 16 17 18 19 20 21 22 23 24 25 26 **27** 28 29 30 31

AUGUST

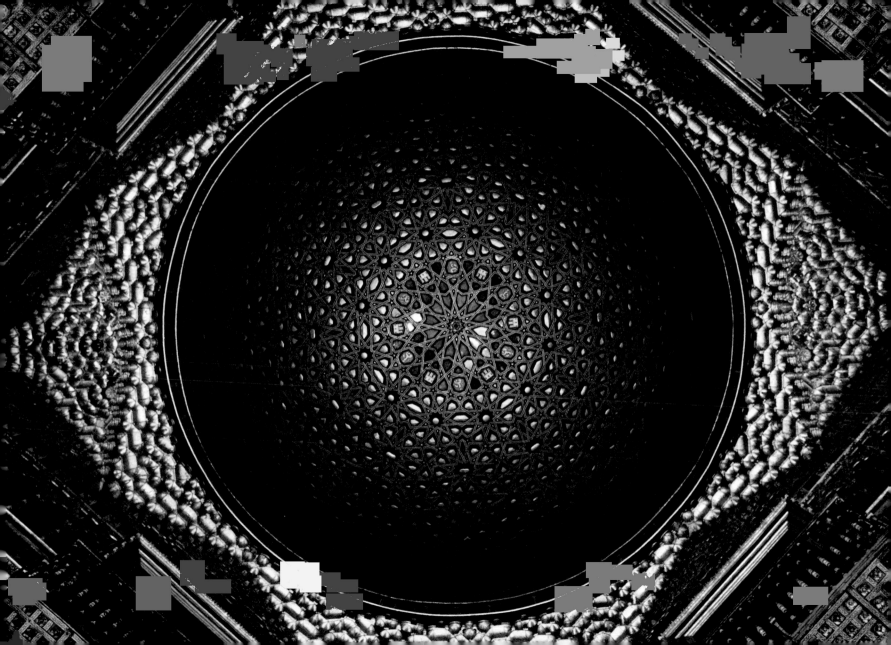

The poet dare help himself wherever he lists, wherever he finds material suited to his work. He may even appropriate entire columns with their carved capitals, if the temple he thus supports be a beautiful one.

Heinrich Heine

Rector's Palace, column capitals, 14th century
Dubrovnik/Croatia

1 2 3 4 5 6 7 8 9 10 11 12 13 14 15 16 17 18 19 20 21 22 23 24 25 26 27 28 29 30 31

AUGUST

You must follow the laws of nature and use quantities of brick, methods of construction, and engineering. But in the end, when the building becomes part of living, it evokes unmeasurable qualities and the spirit of existence takes over.

Louis Kahn

Church of St. Mary, east pediment, 1289–1340
Prenzlau/Germany

1 2 3 4 5 6 7 8 9 10 11 12 13 14 15 16 17 18 19 20 21 22 23 24 25 26 27 28 29 30 31

AUGUST

Architecture would lead us to all
the arts, as it did with earlier men:
but if we despise it and take no note
of how we are housed, the other arts
will have a hard time of it indeed.

William Morris

Groninger Museum, 1990–1994
Alessandro Mendini et al.
Groningen/Netherlands

1 2 3 4 5 6 7 8 9 10 11 12 13 14 15 16 17 18 19 20 21 22 23 24 25 26 27 28 29 30 31

AUGUST

All creative art is magic, is evocation
of the unseen in forms persuasive,
enlightening, familiar and surprising,
for the edification of mankind.

IAC Headquarters, 2004–2007
Frank O. Gehry
New York/USA

Joseph Conrad

1 2 3 4 5 6 7 8 9 10 11 12 13 14 15 16 17 18 19 20 21 22 23 24 25 26 27 28 29 30

SEPTEMBER

The kingdom of colors has within it
multidimensional possibilities only partly to be
reduced to simple order. Each individual color
is a universe in itself. We must therefore content
ourselves with an exposition of fundamentals.

Johannes Itten

National Museum of Fine Arts, stairway, mid-18th century
Valetta/Malta

1 2 3 4 5 6 7 8 9 10 11 12 13 14 15 16 17 18 19 20 21 22 23 24 25 26 27 28 29 30

SEPTEMBER

I didn't want to create a new architectural style
for the Parliament, because I couldn't balance
a building that has to stand for hundreds of
years with ephemeral details. I have tried
modestly and carefully, as is required by art,
to bring a national and unique spirit
to this magnificent medieval style.

Imre Steindl

Hungarian Parliament Building, cupola, 1885–1904
Imre Steindl
Budapest/Hungary

1 2 3 4 5 6 7 8 9 10 11 12 13 14 15 16 17 18 19 20 21 22 23 24 25 26 27 28 29 30

SEPTEMBER

Form does not follow function. Form doesn't originate by itself. It is the great decision of man to make a building into a cube, a pyramid or a sphere.

Hans Hollein and Walter Pichler

Transamerica Pyramid, 1969–1972
William Pereira
San Francisco/USA

1 2 3 4 **5** 6 7 8 9 10 11 12 13 14 15 16 17 18 19 20 21 22 23 24 25 26 27 28 29 30

SEPTEMBER

We build too many walls and
not enough bridges.

Isaac Newton

Ponte Vecchio, 1335–1345
Florence/Italy

1 2 3 4 5 **6** 7 8 9 10 11 12 13 14 15 16 17 18 19 20 21 22 23 24 25 26 27 28 29 30

SEPTEMBER

I say therefore, that architecture,
as well as all other arts, being an
imitatrix of nature, can suffer nothing
that either alienates or deviates from
that which is agreeable to nature.

Andrea Palladio

Château de Chambord, 1519–1544
Chambord/France

1 2 3 4 5 6 7 **8** 9 10 11 12 13 14 15 16 17 18 19 20 21 22 23 24 25 26 27 28 29 30

SEPTEMBER

The *abundance of means* is the
first great danger with which art
has to struggle.

Gottfried Semper

Burj Al Arab Hotel, 1994–1999
W. S. Atkins & Partners
Dubai/United Arab Emirate

1 2 3 4 5 6 7 8 **9** 10 11 12 13 14 15 16 17 18 19 20 21 22 23 24 25 26 27 28 29 30

SEPTEMBER

Propriety will offer us the analogy
of proportions and ornaments;
it will indicate at first glance the motive
of the construction and its use.

Claude Nicolas Ledoux

Royal Saltworks, 1775–1778
Claude Nicolas Ledoux
Arc-et-Senans/France

1 2 3 4 5 6 7 8 9 **10** 11 12 13 14 15 16 17 18 19 20 21 22 23 24 25 26 27 28 29 30

SEPTEMBER

And in the spirit he carried me away
to a great, high mountain and showed
me the holy city Jerusalem coming
down out of heaven from God.
It has the glory of God and a radiance
like a very rare jewel, like jasper,
clear as crystal.

Revelations 21:10-11

Notre-Dame de la Garde, mosaic of the middle portal on the west façade, 1853–1864
Henri-Jacques Espérandieu
Marseilles/France

1 2 3 4 5 6 7 8 9 10 11 12 13 14 15 16 17 18 19 20 21 22 23 24 25 26 27 28 29 30

SEPTEMBER

Insofar as architecture is useful,
it is not art.... Only a very small part
of architecture belongs to art:
the tomb and the monument.

Adolf Loos

Temple of Aesculapius in the Villa Borghese gardens, 1787
Antonio Asprucci
Rome/Italy

1 2 3 4 5 6 7 8 9 10 11 **12** 13 14 15 16 17 18 19 20 21 22 23 24 25 26 27 28 29 30

SEPTEMBER

One day, and probably soon, we need some
recognition of what above all is lacking in our
big cities: quiet and wide, expansive places
for reflection. Places with long, high-ceilinged
cloisters for bad or all too sunny weather …
buildings and sites that would altogether give
expression to the sublimity of thoughtfulness
and of stepping aside.

Friedrich Nietzsche

Punakha Monastery, interior, 1637–1638
Punakha/Bhutan

1 2 3 4 5 6 7 8 9 10 11 12 13 14 15 16 17 18 19 20 21 22 23 24 25 26 27 28 29 30

SEPTEMBER

When the intellectual realm, the realm of ideas,
is in balance with the experiential realm,
the realm of phenomena, form is animated
with meaning. In this balance, architecture has
both intellectual and physical intensity,
with the potential to touch mind, eye, and soul.

Steven Holl

Kiasma Museum of Contemporary Art, 1992–1998
Steven Holl
Helsinki/Finland

1 2 3 4 5 6 7 8 9 10 11 12 13 **14** 15 16 17 18 19 20 21 22 23 24 25 26 27 28 29 30

SEPTEMBER

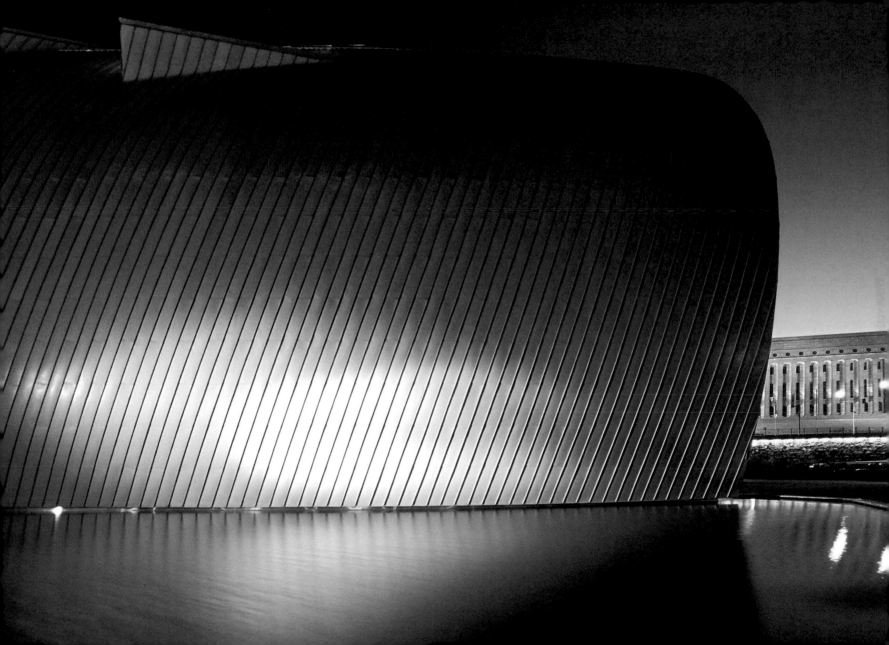

The aim of art is to represent not
the outward appearance of things,
but their inward significance.

Aristotle

Ben Youssef Madrasa in the medina of Marrakech, mosaic detail, 14th century
Marrakech/Morocco

1 2 3 4 5 6 7 8 9 10 11 12 13 14 **15** 16 17 18 19 20 21 22 23 24 25 26 27 28 29 30

SEPTEMBER

Every man's work, whether it be
literature or music or pictures or
architecture or anything else,
is always a portrait of himself.

Samuel Butler

L'Hôtel de Cluny, gargoyle, 1485–1490
Paris/France

1 2 3 4 5 6 7 8 9 10 11 12 13 14 15 **16** 17 18 19 20 21 22 23 24 25 26 27 28 29 30

SEPTEMBER

Let us build ourselves a city, and a
tower with its top in the heavens.

Genesis 11:4

Oriental Pearl Tower, 1992–1995
Jia Huan Cheng
Shanghai/China

1 2 3 4 5 6 7 8 9 10 11 12 13 14 15 16 **17** 18 19 20 21 22 23 24 25 26 27 28 29 30

SEPTEMBER

The man with insight enough
to admit his limitations comes nearest
to perfection.

Johann Wolfgang von Goethe

Borobudur Temple, 750–850
Java/Indonesia

1 2 3 4 5 6 7 8 9 10 11 12 13 14 15 16 17 18 19 20 21 22 23 24 25 26 27 28 29 30

SEPTEMBER

You should be bold. You should have
the courage to be utopian and think
out certain things which may be
desirable for men to have.

Walter Gropius

Gellért Baths, 1912–1918
Budapest/Hungary

1 2 3 4 5 6 7 8 9 10 11 12 13 14 15 16 17 18 **19** 20 21 22 23 24 25 26 27 28 29 30

SEPTEMBER

Him I consider the architect, who by
sure and wonderful reason and
method, knows both how to devise
through his own mind and energy,
and to realize by construction,
whatever can be most beautifully fitted
out for the noble needs of man.

Leon Battista Alberti

Maison de la Culture du Havre ("Le Volcan"), 1972–1978
Oscar Niemeyer
Le Havre/France

1 2 3 4 5 6 7 8 9 10 11 12 13 14 15 16 17 18 19 20 21 22 23 24 25 26 27 28 29 30

SEPTEMBER

Bright is the noble work; but being
nobly bright, the work should brighten
the minds, so that that they may travel.

Abbot Suger of St. Denis

Poitiers Cathedral (Saint-Pierre de Poitiers), ca. 1080–1150
Poitiers/France

1 2 3 4 5 6 7 8 9 10 11 12 13 14 15 16 17 18 19 20 21 22 23 24 25 26 27 28 29 30

SEPTEMBER

Of pleasures, those which occur
most rarely give the most delight.

Epictetus

Fish sculpture, Olympic Harbor, detail, 1992
Frank O. Gehry
Barcelona/Spain

1 2 3 4 5 6 7 8 9 10 11 12 13 14 15 16 17 18 19 20 21 22 23 24 25 26 27 28 29 30

SEPTEMBER

What distinguishes architecture from painting
and sculpture is its spatial quality. In this,
and only in this, no other artist can emulate
the architect … history of architecture
is primarily a history of man shaping space.

Nikolaus Pevsner

Monastery Church of Madonna delle Grazie, 1390–1549
Certosa di Pavia/Italy

1 2 3 4 5 6 7 8 9 10 11 12 13 14 15 16 17 18 19 20 21 22 23 24 25 26 27 28 29 30

SEPTEMBER

These high-pitched gables,
these Baroque cupolas, spires,
and pinnacles, neither are, nor desire
to be, related with anything in Nature.

Oswald Spengler

St. Nicolas Cathedral, roof domes, 1903–1906
Nice/France

1 2 3 4 5 6 7 8 9 10 11 12 13 14 15 16 17 18 19 20 21 22 23 **24** 25 26 27 28 29 30

SEPTEMBER

History fades into fable; fact becomes clouded
with doubt and controversy; the inscription
moulders from the tablet: the statue falls from
the pedestal. Columns, arches, pyramids,
what are they but heaps of sand; and their
epitaphs, but characters written in the dust?

Washington Irving

Olympia, Ionic column capitals, 4th century BCE
Olympia/Greece

1 2 3 4 5 6 7 8 9 10 11 12 13 14 15 16 17 18 19 20 21 22 23 24 25 26 27 28 29 30

SEPTEMBER

Strength without agility is a mere mass.

Fernando Pessoa

Eiffel Tower, 1887–1889
Gustave Eiffel
Paris/France

1 2 3 4 5 6 7 8 9 10 11 12 13 14 15 16 17 18 19 20 21 22 23 24 25 26 27 28 29 30

SEPTEMBER

We should erect our buildings naked,
and let it be quite completed before
we begin to dress it with ornament.

Leon Battista Alberti

Beloselsky-Belozersky Palace, 1846–1848
Andrei Stackenschneider
St. Petersburg/Russia

1 2 3 4 5 6 7 8 9 10 11 12 13 14 15 16 17 18 19 20 21 22 23 24 25 26 27 28 29 30

SEPTEMBER

An enormous spherical dome …
seems not to be founded on solid
masonry, but to be suspended from
heaven by that golden chain.

Hagia Sophia, 532–537
Anthemius of Tralles
Istanbul/Turkey

Procopius

1 2 3 4 5 6 7 8 9 10 11 12 13 14 15 16 17 18 19 20 21 22 23 24 25 26 27 28 29 30

SEPTEMBER

It seems incredible that the size
of a building alone embodies an
ideological program, independent
of the will of its architects.

Rem Koolhaas

Seagram Building, 1957
Philip Johnson
New York/USA

1 2 3 4 5 6 7 8 9 10 11 12 13 14 15 16 17 18 19 20 21 22 23 24 25 26 27 28 29 30

SEPTEMBER

It is the same in architecture as in all other arts: its principles are founded on simple nature, and nature's process clearly indicates its rules.

Marc-Antoine Laugier

Hradčany (Prague Castle), Vladislav Hall, 1490–1502
Prague/Czech Republic

1 2 3 4 5 6 7 8 9 10 11 12 13 14 15 16 17 18 19 20 21 22 23 24 25 26 27 28 29 30

SEPTEMBER

I think that architects and designers
produce interesting objects when
the client is intelligent.

Pierluigi Cerri

Museum of the Fondazione Arnaldo Pomodoro, interior view, 2005
Pierluigi Cerri, Alessandro Colombo
Milan/Italy

1 2 3 4 5 6 7 8 9 10 11 12 13 14 15 16 17 18 19 20 21 22 23 24 25 26 27 28 29 30 31

OCTOBER

That holy dream – that holy dream,
While all the world were chiding,
Hath cheered me as a lovely beam
A lonely spirit guiding.

Edgar Allan Poe

Palais Idéal, 1879–1912
Ferdinand Cheval
Hauterives/France

1 2 3 4 5 6 7 8 9 10 11 12 13 14 15 16 17 18 19 20 21 22 23 24 25 26 27 28 29 30 31

OCTOBER

DÉFENSE

Afin d'éviter les accidents les parents
sont priés de surveiller leurs enfants

DE RIEN

TOUCHER

DIX MILLE JOURNÉES
130 MILLE HEURES
33 ANS D'EPREUVES
PLUS OPINIATRE
QUE MOI SE METTE
A L'ŒUVRE

What we now call "monumental architecture" is first of all the expression of power, and that power exhibits itself in the assemblage of costly building materials and of all the resources of art.

Lewis Mumford

Brandenburg Gate, 1788–1791
Carl Gotthard Langhans
Berlin/Germany

1 2 3 4 5 6 7 8 9 10 11 12 13 14 15 16 17 18 19 20 21 22 23 24 25 26 27 28 29 30 31

OCTOBER

Cities are, especially old cities,
are a bit like human bodies,
they are very vulnerable. They need
to change by using their internal
resource and their internal energy
more than by just making surgery.

Renzo Piano

Padre Pio Pilgrimage Church, 1991–2004
Renzo Piano
San Giovanni Rotondo/Italy

1 2 3 4 5 6 7 8 9 10 11 12 13 14 15 16 17 18 19 20 21 22 23 24 25 26 27 28 29 30 31

OCTOBER

In Architecture as in all other Operative
Arts, the end must direct the Operation.
The end is to build well.
Well building hath three Conditions.
Commodity, Firmness, and Delight.

Henry Wotton

The Westin New York at Times Square, 2002
Arquitectonica
New York/USA

1 2 3 4 5 6 7 8 9 10 11 12 13 14 15 16 17 18 19 20 21 22 23 24 25 26 27 28 29 30 31

OCTOBER

We have a great selfishness that chills
like east winds the world, the whole
human family is bathed with an
element of love like a fine ether.

Ralph Waldo Emerson

Abbey Church of Sainte-Foy, tympanum of the western portal, before 1130
Aveyron/France

1 2 3 4 5 **6** 7 8 9 10 11 12 13 14 15 16 17 18 19 20 21 22 23 24 25 26 27 28 29 30 31

OCTOBER

All architecture is what you do to it
when you look upon it.

Walt Whitman

Potala Palace, since the 17th century
Lhasa/Tibet

1 2 3 4 5 6 7 8 9 10 11 12 13 14 15 16 17 18 19 20 21 22 23 24 25 26 27 28 29 30 31

OCTOBER

Truly art lies in Nature;
he who can extract it has attained art.

Hotel on Rivington, 2005
Grzywinski Pons
New York/USA

Albrecht Dürer

1 2 3 4 5 6 7 **8** 9 10 11 12 13 14 15 16 17 18 19 20 21 22 23 24 25 26 27 28 29 30 31

OCTOBER

Thou art my refuge,
a strong tower against the enemy.

Psalm 61:4

Munich Frauenkirche (Church of Our Lady), 1468–1488
Jörg von Halsbach
Munich/Germany

1 2 3 4 5 6 7 8 9 10 11 12 13 14 15 16 17 18 19 20 21 22 23 24 25 26 27 28 29 30 31

OCTOBER

Self-sufficiency is the greatest
of all wealth.

Epicurus

La Vieille Bourse (old mercantile exchange), window detail, 1653
Julien Destrée
Lille/France

1 2 3 4 5 6 7 8 9 **10** 11 12 13 14 15 16 17 18 19 20 21 22 23 24 25 26 27 28 29 30 31

OCTOBER

It is impossible to understand Art and
the glory of its history without avowing
religious spirituality and the mythical
roots that lead us to the very reason of
being of the artistic phenomenon.

Luis Barragán

Puebla Cathedral, tabernacle, 1575–1649
Manuel Tolsá
Puebla/Mexico

1 2 3 4 5 6 7 8 9 10 11 12 13 14 15 16 17 18 19 20 21 22 23 24 25 26 27 28 29 30 31

OCTOBER

Sometimes, perhaps, it was the monk,
the ploughman's brother; oftenest his other
brother, the village carpenter, smith, mason,
what not – "a common fellow," whose
common everyday labour fashioned works
that are to-day the wonder and despair of
many a hard-working "cultivated" architect.

William Morris

Greek Orthodox Church, undated
Oia/Santorini/Greece

1 2 3 4 5 6 7 8 9 10 11 12 13 14 15 16 17 18 19 20 21 22 23 24 25 26 27 28 29 30 31

OCTOBER

The whole visible universe is but a
storehouse of images and signs to
which the imagination will give a
relative place and value; it is a sort of
pasture which the imagination must
digest and transform.

Charles Baudelaire

Reims Cathedral (Notre-Dame de Reims), west portal, 1212–1300
Reims/France

1 2 3 4 5 6 7 8 9 10 11 12 **13** 14 15 16 17 18 19 20 21 22 23 24 25 26 27 28 29 30 31

OCTOBER

Do you wish to rise?
Begin by descending. You plan a tower
that will pierce the clouds?
Lay first the foundation of humility.

St. Augustine

Bank of China, 1987–1989
I. M. Pei & Partners
Hong Kong/China

1 2 3 4 5 6 7 8 9 10 11 12 13 14 15 16 17 18 19 20 21 22 23 24 25 26 27 28 29 30 31

OCTOBER

Everyone should be free to choose for
himself the foundations of his creed,
and that faith should be judged
only by its fruits.

Baruch Spinoza

Angkor Wat temple complex, reliefs, 12th century
Angkor Wat/Cambodia

1 2 3 4 5 6 7 8 9 10 11 12 13 14 **15** 16 17 18 19 20 21 22 23 24 25 26 27 28 29 30 31

OCTOBER

Architecture is the continuation of
nature in her constructive activity.
This activity is conducted through
a natural product: Mankind.

Karl Friedrich Schinkel

Dwellings of the Tellem in the Bandiagara cliffs, 11th–14th century
Bandiagara/Mali

1 2 3 4 5 6 7 8 9 10 11 12 13 14 15 16 17 18 19 20 21 22 23 24 25 26 27 28 29 30 31

OCTOBER

The noblest function of an object
is to be contemplated.

Miguel de Unamuno

Hotel Marqués de Riscal, 2003–2006
Frank O. Gehry
Elciego/Spain

1 2 3 4 5 6 7 8 9 10 11 12 13 14 15 16 **17** 18 19 20 21 22 23 24 25 26 27 28 29 30 31

OCTOBER

In the great inconstancy and crowd
of events, nothing is certain except
the past.

Seneca

Rock city of Petra, 3rd century BCE to 663 CE
Petra/Jordan

1 2 3 4 5 6 7 8 9 10 11 12 13 14 15 16 17 18 19 20 21 22 23 24 25 26 27 28 29 30 31

OCTOBER

All things fall and are built again,
And those that build them again
are gay.

William Butler Yeats

World Trade Center, 1966–1973, 2001 (destroyed)
Minoru Yamasaki
New York/USA

1 2 3 4 5 6 7 8 9 10 11 12 13 14 15 16 17 18 **19** 20 21 22 23 24 25 26 27 28 29 30 31

OCTOBER

Architecture exhibits the greatest extent of the
difference from nature which may exist in works
of art. It involves all the powers of design,
and is sculpture and painting inclusively.
It shows the greatness of man, and should
at the same time teach him humility.

Samuel Taylor Coleridge

Albi Cathedral (Sainte-Cécile d'Albi), choir enclosure, 1282–1482
Albi/France

1 2 3 4 5 6 7 8 9 10 11 12 13 14 15 16 17 18 19 20 21 22 23 24 25 26 27 28 29 30 31

OCTOBER

The goal of the design process is not to achieve a specific form, but to arrive at the most comprehensive and precise architectural definition of a specific tool for the purpose of "improving life."

Walter Nägeli

Braun AG Headquarters, 1988
Wilford, Stirling, Nägeli
Melsungen/Germany

1 2 3 4 5 6 7 8 9 10 11 12 13 14 15 16 17 18 19 20 21 22 23 24 25 26 27 28 29 30 31

OCTOBER

But it isn't just a matter of faith,
but of faith and works.

St. Augustine

Abbey of Thoronet, cloister, 1160–1180
Le Thoronet/France

1 2 3 4 5 6 7 8 9 10 11 12 13 14 15 16 17 18 19 20 21 22 23 24 25 26 27 28 29 30 31

OCTOBER

Style in architecture is the peculiar
form that expression takes under the
influence of climate and materials
at command.

Owen Jones

Hagia Sophia, 532–537
Anthemius of Tralles
Istanbul/Turkey

1 2 3 4 5 6 7 8 9 10 11 12 13 14 15 16 17 18 19 20 21 22 23 24 25 26 27 28 29 30 31

OCTOBER

I believe in intuition and inspiration.
Imagination is more important than
knowledge. For knowledge is limited,
whereas imagination embraces the
entire world, stimulating progress,
giving birth to evolution.

Albert Einstein

Atomium, 1958
André Waterkeyn
Brussels/Belgium

1 2 3 4 5 6 7 8 9 10 11 12 13 14 15 16 17 18 19 20 21 22 23 24 25 26 27 28 29 30 31

OCTOBER

One day houses will be turned inside
out like gloves.

Paul Éluard

Centre Georges Pompidou, 1971–1977
Renzo Piano, Richard Rogers, Gianfranco Franchini
Paris/France

1 2 3 4 5 6 7 8 9 10 11 12 13 14 15 16 17 18 19 20 21 22 23 24 25 **26** 27 28 29 30 31

OCTOBER

These marbles, the works of the
dreamers and idealists of old, live on,
leading and pointing to good.

Herman Melville

Basilica of St. Peter, east façade with Jesus and apostles, 1607–1614
Carlo Maderno
Rome/Italy

1 2 3 4 5 6 7 8 9 10 11 12 13 14 15 16 17 18 19 20 21 22 23 24 25 26 27 28 29 30 31

OCTOBER

PAVLVS·V·BVRGHESIVS·ROMANVS·PONT·MAX·AN·MD

What heavenly notes burst
on my ravished ears,
What beauteous spirits
met my dazzled eye!

Percy Bysshe Shelley

Teatro alla Scala, 2001–2004
Mario Botta
Milan/Italy

1 2 3 4 5 6 7 8 9 10 11 12 13 14 15 16 17 18 19 20 21 22 23 24 25 26 27 28 29 30 31

OCTOBER

History is the witness that testifies to
the passing of time; it illumines reality,
vitalizes memory, provides guidance
in daily life and brings us tidings
of antiquity

Cicero

Roman Theater, ca. 200 CE
Sabratha/Libya

1 2 3 4 5 6 7 8 9 10 11 12 13 14 15 16 17 18 19 20 21 22 23 24 25 26 27 28 29 30 31

OCTOBER

Men are always building better
than they know.

Rudyard Kipling

Diwan-i-Khas (private audience hall), Red Fort, 1639
Delhi/India

1 2 3 4 5 6 7 8 9 10 11 12 13 14 15 16 17 18 19 20 21 22 23 24 25 26 27 28 29 30 31

OCTOBER

The age demanded an image
Of its accelerated grimace,
Something for the modern stage
Not, at any rate, an Attic grace.

Ezra Pound

American Radiator Building, 1924
Raymond Hood and André Fouilhoux
New York/USA

1 2 3 4 5 6 7 8 9 10 11 12 13 14 15 16 17 18 19 20 21 22 23 24 25 26 27 28 29 30 31

OCTOBER

A creator is not in advance of his
generation but he is the first of his
contemporaries to be conscious of
what is happening to his generation.

Gertrude Stein

Ciudad Grupo Santander, 2005
Kevin Roche
Madrid/Spain

1 2 3 4 5 6 7 8 9 10 11 12 13 14 15 16 17 18 19 20 21 22 23 24 25 26 27 28 29 30

NOVEMBER

Ornamentation is no less foreign
to virtue, which is the strength and
vigor of the soul.

Jean-Jacques Rousseau

Reims Cathedral (Notre-Dame de Reims), west portal, 1211–1311
Reims/France

1 2 3 4 5 6 7 8 9 10 11 12 13 14 15 16 17 18 19 20 21 22 23 24 25 26 27 28 29 30

NOVEMBER

The territory of architecture is the
territory of a geographical memory.
In a site there is always a culture,
a memory, which needs to be
interpreted in a contemporary
condition.

Petra Winery, 2001–2003
Mario Botta
Suvereto/Italy

Mario Botta

1 2 **3** 4 5 6 7 8 9 10 11 12 13 14 15 16 17 18 19 20 21 22 23 24 25 26 27 28 29 30

NOVEMBER

Then rose the Builders;
First the Architect divine his plan
Unfolds, The wondrous scaffold
reard all round the infinite
Quadrangular the building rose
the heavens squared by a line.

William Blake

Palatine Chapel, octagonal dome, end of 8th century
Aachen/Germany

1 2 3 4 5 6 7 8 9 10 11 12 13 14 15 16 17 18 19 20 21 22 23 24 25 26 27 28 29 30

NOVEMBER

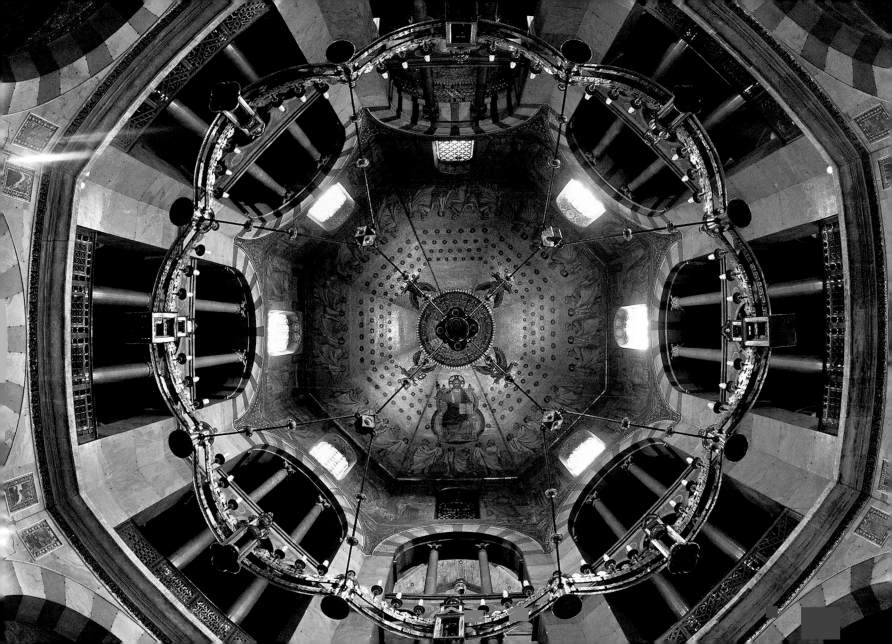

If Nature had been comfortable,
mankind would never have invented
architecture, and I prefer houses
to the open air.

Oscar Wilde

Chesa Futura apartment building, 2002
Norman Foster
St. Moritz/Switzerland

5

1 2 3 4 5 6 7 8 9 10 11 12 13 14 15 16 17 18 19 20 21 22 23 24 25 26 27 28 29 30

NOVEMBER

What sculpture is to a block of marble,
education is to the soul.

Joseph Addison

University of Oxford, after 1474
Oxford/England

1 2 3 4 5 6 7 8 9 10 11 12 13 14 15 16 17 18 19 20 21 22 23 24 25 26 27 28 29 30

NOVEMBER

Because city and landscape are
caught today in a contradictory dual
movement that alternates between
unity and dispersion, many of my
other projects are underpinned,
on the contrary, by a quest for an
"attachment to landscape."

Paul Andreu

National Centre for the Performing Arts ("The Egg"), 2001–2008
Paul Andreu
Beijing/China

1 2 3 4 5 6 7 **8** 9 10 11 12 13 14 15 16 17 18 19 20 21 22 23 24 25 26 27 28 29 30

NOVEMBER

Earth proudly wears the Parthenon
As the best gem upon her zone.

Ralph Waldo Emerson

Parthenon, gable frieze, 447–433 BCE
Iktinos, Kallikrates
Athens/Greece

1 2 3 4 5 6 7 8 9 10 11 12 13 14 15 16 17 18 19 20 21 22 23 24 25 26 27 28 29 30

NOVEMBER

As I have said already, I regard honest construction in simplified form as the correct principle on which we should work in the short term.

Henrik Petrus Berlage

Hearst Tower, 2004
Norman Foster
New York/USA

1 2 3 4 5 6 7 8 9 **10** 11 12 13 14 15 16 17 18 19 20 21 22 23 24 25 26 27 28 29 30

NOVEMBER

You must live in the present,
launch yourself on every wave,
find your eternity in each moment.

Henry David Thoreau

Superstudio Più, 2000
Milan/Italy

1 2 3 4 5 6 7 8 9 10 11 12 13 14 15 16 17 18 19 20 21 22 23 24 25 26 27 28 29 30

NOVEMBER

The ornaments of the capitals are
the words of Sacred Scripture,
to the meditation and observance
of which we are bound.

William Durandus

Notre-Dame de la Garde, façade detail, 1853–1864
Henri-Jacques Espérandieu
Marseilles/France

1 2 3 4 5 6 7 8 9 10 11 12 13 14 15 16 17 18 19 20 21 22 23 24 25 26 27 28 29 30

NOVEMBER

The simplification of anything
is always sensational.

G. K. Chesterton

Master House, staircase, 1925–1926
Walter Gropius
Dessau/Germany

1 2 3 4 5 6 7 8 9 10 11 12 13 14 15 16 17 18 19 20 21 22 23 24 25 26 27 28 29 30

NOVEMBER

Uniformity and proportions are very
pleasing to the eye;
and 'tis observable that free-stone,
like a fair complexion, grows old,
whilst bricks keep their beauty longest.

Thomas Fuller

Guîtres Abbey (Notre-Dame de Guîtres), west portal, 12th–17th century
Guîtres/France

1 2 3 4 5 6 7 8 9 10 11 12 13 14 15 16 17 18 19 20 21 22 23 24 25 26 27 28 29 30

NOVEMBER

Architecture lives and survives because
of its beauty, because it seduces,
animates and even inspires people,
because it is matter and because
it can – if only sometimes – transcend
matter.

Jacques Herzog

IKMZ (Centre for Information, Communication and Media) at BTU Cottbus, Library,
interior stairs, 1998–2004
Herzog & de Meuron
Cottbus/Germany

1 2 3 4 5 6 7 8 9 10 11 12 13 14 **15** 16 17 18 19 20 21 22 23 24 25 26 27 28 29 30

NOVEMBER

In architecture we are not concerned
with beauty. If we want beauty
then we want it less in form or
proportion than in a sensual beauty
of fundamental power.

Hans Hollein and Walter Pichler

Palais de Justice, 1951
Le Corbusier
Chandigarh/India

1 2 3 4 5 6 7 8 9 10 11 12 13 14 15 16 17 18 19 20 21 22 23 24 25 26 27 28 29 30

NOVEMBER

It is written on the arched sky.
It looks out from every star.
It is the poetry of Nature.
It is that which uplifts the spirit within us.

John Ruskin

Samode Palace Hotel, detail, 19th century
Samode/India

1 2 3 4 5 6 7 8 9 10 11 12 13 14 15 16 17 18 19 20 21 22 23 24 25 26 27 28 29 30

NOVEMBER

The time is past when the church possessed a monopoly on reflection, when the *vita contemplative* always had to be first of all a *vita religiosa*.

Friedrich Nietzsche

National Gallery of Canada, 1988
Moshe Safdie
Ottawa/Canada

1 2 3 4 5 6 7 8 9 10 11 12 13 14 15 16 17 **18** 19 20 21 22 23 24 25 26 27 28 29 30

NOVEMBER

Beauty in things exists in the mind
which contemplates them.

David Hume

Erdene Zuu Monastery, 1586
Karakorum/Mongolia/China

1 2 3 4 5 6 7 8 9 10 11 12 13 14 15 16 17 18 19 20 21 22 23 24 25 26 27 28 29 30

NOVEMBER

I like the silent church
before the service begins,
better than any preaching.

Ralph Waldo Emerson

Laon Cathedral (Notre-Dame de Laon), central nave, 1170–1235
Laon/France

1 2 3 4 5 6 7 8 9 10 11 12 13 14 15 16 17 18 19 20 21 22 23 24 25 26 27 28 29 30

NOVEMBER

A crowd of illusions form the decoration
of the building of which nature has laid
the foundations.

Tempodrom, roof structure, 2000–2001
Meinhard von Gerkan
Berlin/Germany

Voltaire

1 2 3 4 5 6 7 8 9 10 11 12 13 14 15 16 17 18 19 20 21 22 23 24 25 26 27 28 29 30

NOVEMBER

These stones – alas! these grey stones –
are they all –
All of the famed, and the colossal left
By the corrosive Hours to Fate and me?

Edgar Allan Poe

Coliseum, 72–80 CE
Rome/Italy

1 2 3 4 5 6 7 8 9 10 11 12 13 14 15 16 17 18 19 20 21 22 23 24 25 26 27 28 29 30

NOVEMBER

The union of the mathematician with
the poet, fervor with measure, passion
with correctness, this surely is the ideal.

William James

Qutb Minar, 1200–1236
Delhi/India

1 2 3 4 5 6 7 8 9 10 11 12 13 14 15 16 17 18 19 20 21 22 23 24 25 26 27 28 29 30

NOVEMBER

Light (God's eldest daughter)
is a principal beauty in a building;
yet it shines out alike from all parts
of the heavens.

Thomas Fuller

Al-Fateh Mosque, Detail, 1990
Manama/Bahrain

1 2 3 4 5 6 7 8 9 10 11 12 13 14 15 16 17 18 19 20 21 22 23 24 25 26 27 28 29 30

NOVEMBER

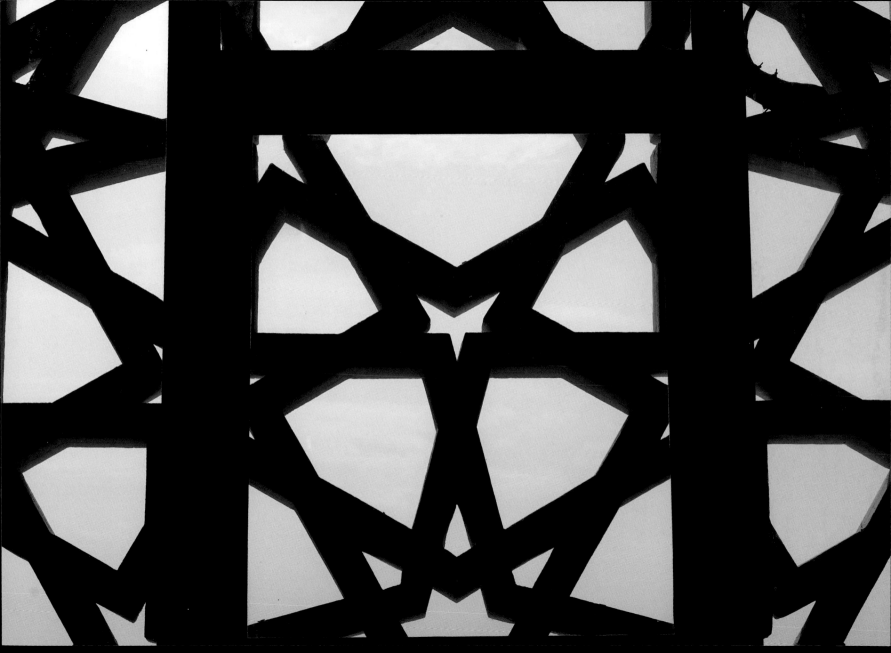

Architecture is the masterly, correct,
and magnificent play of masses
brought together in light.

Le Corbusier

Süleymaniye Mosque, interior, 1550–1557
Sinan
Istanbul/Turkey

1 2 3 4 5 6 7 8 9 10 11 12 13 14 15 16 17 18 19 20 21 22 23 24 25 26 27 28 29 30

NOVEMBER

In a building, pride, victory over
gravity, the will to power should make
themselves visible; architecture is a kind
of power-eloquence in forms, at times
persuading, even flattering, at times
simply commanding.

Friedrich Nietzsche

Arc de Triomphe, 1806–1836
Jean-François Chalgrin
Paris/France

1 2 3 4 5 6 7 8 9 10 11 12 13 14 15 16 17 18 19 20 21 22 23 24 25 26 27 28 29 30

NOVEMBER

I will go lose myself, and wander up
and down to view the city.

William Shakespeare

Itchan Kala (walled city), 18th–19th century
Khiva/Uzbekistan

1 2 3 4 5 6 7 8 9 10 11 12 13 14 15 16 17 18 19 20 21 22 23 24 25 26 27 28 29 30

NOVEMBER

Tell me you stones, O speak,
you towering palaces!
Streets, say a word! Spirit of this place,
are you dumb?
All things are alive in your sacred walls
Eternal Rome, it's only for me all is still.

Johann Wolfgang von Goethe

Church Santi Luca e Martina, near the Roman Forum, 1634–1635
Ottaviano Mascherino, Pietro da Cortona
Rome/Italy

1 2 3 4 5 6 7 8 9 10 11 12 13 14 15 16 17 18 19 20 21 22 23 24 25 26 27 28 29 30

NOVEMBER

Exhibit the unadorned and embrace
the uncarved block,
Have little thought of self and
as few desires as possible.

Lao Tzu

Bayonne Cathedral (Sainte-Marie de Bayonne), 1213 to 15th century
Bayonne/France

1 2 3 4 5 6 7 8 9 10 11 12 13 14 15 16 17 18 19 20 21 22 23 24 25 26 27 28 29 30

NOVEMBER

I am more interested in movement
that is relevant all the way through
the motion. Does a flower have to be
closed or opened? No. Any part of the
opening or closing motion is beautiful.

Santiago Calatrava

Auditorium of Tenerife, exterior view, 1989–2003
Santiago Calatrava
Santa Cruz/Spain

1 2 3 4 5 6 7 8 9 10 11 12 13 14 15 16 17 18 19 20 21 22 23 24 25 26 27 28 29 30

NOVEMBER

Architecture has many facets … and one of
the great skills that anyone can develop as an
aspiring architect is to be able to deal with
philosophical and political issues, as well as to
be ready to know what to do so that the roof
doesn't leak.

Bernard Tschumi

Cologne City Hall, 1567–1571
Cornelis Floris and Wilhelm Vernukken
Cologne/Germany

1 2 3 4 5 6 7 8 9 10 11 12 13 14 15 16 17 18 19 20 21 22 23 24 25 26 27 28 29 30 31

DECEMBER

It is architecture that pioneers the way
for the adequate realisation of the
God, and in this its service bestows
hard toil upon existing nature, in
order to disentangle it from the jingle
of finitude and the abortiveness
of change.

G. W. F. Hegel

Dresden Frauenkirche (Church of Our Lady), from 1702
Georg Bähr
Dresden/Germany

1 2 3 4 5 6 7 8 9 10 11 12 13 14 15 16 17 18 19 20 21 22 23 24 25 26 27 28 29 30 31

DECEMBER

Consistency is found in that work
whose whole and detail are suitable
to the occasion. It arises from
circumstance, custom, and nature.

Vitruvius

Sony Center at Potsdamer Platz, 1996–2000
Helmut Jahn
Berlin/Germany

1 2 3 4 5 6 7 8 9 10 11 12 13 14 15 16 17 18 19 20 21 22 23 24 25 26 27 28 29 30 31

DECEMBER

The decorative arts that are widespread on
this earth must advance in step with political
economy. Do you wish to give them greater
scope? Do you wish their expansion to the
greatest number? Then you must awaken
common interests, and then all men
will be driven to help in their progression.

Claude Nicolas Ledoux

Palace of Versailles, courtyard, 1631–1780
Versailles/France

1 2 3 4 5 6 7 8 9 10 11 12 13 14 15 16 17 18 19 20 21 22 23 24 25 26 27 28 29 30 31

DECEMBER

The world is a looking-glass,
and gives back to every man
the reflection of his own face.

William Makepeace Thackeray

Swiss Re-Tower, façade, 2001–2004
Ken Shuttleworth, Norman Foster
London/England

1 2 3 4 5 6 7 8 9 10 11 12 13 14 15 16 17 18 19 20 21 22 23 24 25 26 27 28 29 30 31

DECEMBER

Whatever is in architecture fair or
beautiful, is imitated from natural forms.

John Ruskin

Jiayuguan Fortress, 1372–1539
Jiayuguan/China

1 2 3 4 5 **6** 7 8 9 10 11 12 13 14 15 16 17 18 19 20 21 22 23 24 25 26 27 28 29 30 31

DECEMBER

Architecture in itself conveys this idea
of limiting space. It's a limit between
the finite and the infinite. From this
point of view, all architecture is sacred.

Mario Botta

Hassan II Mosque, 1987–1993
Casablanca/Morocco

1 2 3 4 5 6 7 8 9 10 11 12 13 14 15 16 17 18 19 20 21 22 23 24 25 26 27 28 29 30 31

DECEMBER

In the greenest of our valleys
By good angels tenanted,
Once a fair and stately palace –
Radiant palace – reared its head.

Edgar Allan Poe

Château de Chambord, roof detail, 1519–1544
Chambord/France

8

1 2 3 4 5 6 7 8 9 10 11 12 13 14 15 16 17 18 19 20 21 22 23 24 25 26 27 28 29 30 31

DECEMBER

Every noble work is at first "impossible."
In very truth, for every noble work
the possibilities will lie diffused
through Immensity.

Thomas Carlyle

Basilica of San Vitale, 522–547
Ravenna/Italy

9

1 2 3 4 5 6 7 8 9 10 11 12 13 14 15 16 17 18 19 20 21 22 23 24 25 26 27 28 29 30 31

DECEMBER

In an architectural Order only
the column, the entablature and
the pediment may form an essential
part of its composition. If each of
these parts is suitably placed and
suitably formed, nothing else need
be added to make the work perfect.

Marc-Antoine Laugier

La Vieille Charité, 1671–1704
Pierre Puget
Marseilles/France

1 2 3 4 5 6 7 8 9 10 11 12 13 14 15 16 17 18 19 20 21 22 23 24 25 26 27 28 29 30 31

DECEMBER

If I were to sum up the whole question,
I would say that sacred buildings
ought to be so designed that nothing
further may be added to enhance
their majesty or cause greater
admiration for their beauty.

Leon Battista Albert

Aachen Cathedral, ca. 790–800
Aachen/Germany

1 2 3 4 5 6 7 8 9 10 11 12 13 14 15 16 17 18 19 20 21 22 23 24 25 26 27 28 29 30 31

DECEMBER

Any great work of art … revives and readapts
time and space, and the measure of its
success is the extent to which it makes you an
inhabitant of that world – the extent to which
it invites you in and lets you breathe its strange,
special air.

Leonard Bernstein

Opera of El Palau de les Arts Reina Sofía, 1991–2006
Santiago Calatrava
Valencia/Spain

1 2 3 4 5 6 7 8 9 10 11 12 13 14 15 16 17 18 19 20 21 22 23 24 25 26 27 28 29 30 31

DECEMBER

Write the bad things that are done
to you in sand, but write the good
things that happen to you
on a piece of marble.

Arabic proverb

Alhambra, Hall of the Abencerrajes, stucco decoration, 15th century
Granada/Spain

1 2 3 4 5 6 7 8 9 10 11 12 **13** 14 15 16 17 18 19 20 21 22 23 24 25 26 27 28 29 30 31

DECEMBER

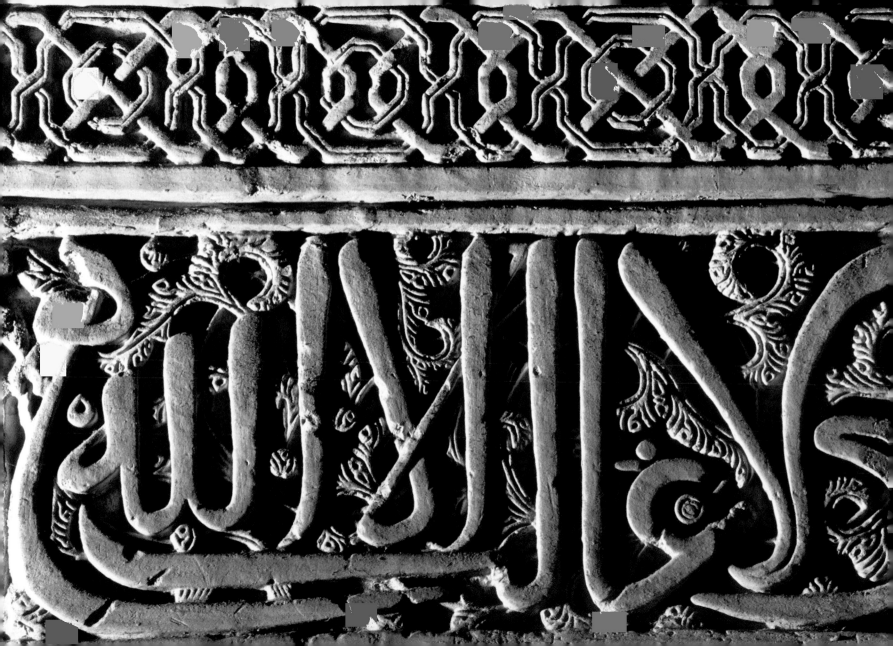

My research is always around the idea
of specificity and I don't like to repeat
the same vocabulary or to do the
same architecture on every spot on
the earth.

Institut du Monde Arabe, 1987
Jean Nouvel, Pierre Soria and Architecture Studio
Paris/France

Jean Nouvel

1 2 3 4 5 6 7 8 9 10 11 12 13 **14** 15 16 17 18 19 20 21 22 23 24 25 26 27 28 29 30 31

DECEMBER

For thon, O Spring! canot renovate
All that high God did first create.
Be still his arms and architect, Rebuild
the ruin, mend defect.

Ralph Waldo Emerson

St. Michael's Golden-Domed Monastery, façade, 1108–1760
Sviatopolk II Iziaslavich et al.
Kiev/Ukraine

1 2 3 4 5 6 7 8 9 10 11 12 13 14 **15** 16 17 18 19 20 21 22 23 24 25 26 27 28 29 30 31

DECEMBER

In the elder days of Art,
Builders wrought with greatest care
Each minute and unseen part;
For the gods see everywhere.

Henry Wadsworth Longfellow

St. Paul's Cathedral, 1677–1708
Christopher Wren
London/England

1 2 3 4 5 6 7 8 9 10 11 12 13 14 15 **16** 17 18 19 20 21 22 23 24 25 26 27 28 29 30 31

DECEMBER

We want no new style of architecture,
the forms already known to us
are good enough for us,
and far better than any of us.

John Ruskin

The Helmsley Building, 1929
Warren & Wetmore
New York/USA

1 2 3 4 5 6 7 8 9 10 11 12 13 14 15 16 17 18 19 20 21 22 23 24 25 26 27 28 29 30 31

DECEMBER

Architecture consists in doing things
right. Science consists in inquiring
how to do things right.

Bernard Maybeck

Phœno Science Center, coat check area and benches, 2005
Zaha Hadid
Wolfsburg/Germany

1 2 3 4 5 6 7 8 9 10 11 12 13 14 15 16 17 **18** 19 20 21 22 23 24 25 26 27 28 29 30 31

DECEMBER

The Middle Ages put the idea before
all doctrine or tradition, following the
idea fanatically, often blindly.

Eugène-Emmanuel Viollet-le-Duc

Strasbourg Cathedral (Notre-Dame-de-Strasbourg), 1176–1439
Strasbourg/France

1 2 3 4 5 6 7 8 9 10 11 12 13 14 15 16 17 18 **19** 20 21 22 23 24 25 26 27 28 29 30 31

DECEMBER

The often made comparison of music
and architecture rests upon the fact
that these arts, more directly than
others, exemplify organic recurrences
effected by cumulative relationships
rather by repetition of units.

John Dewey

Casa da Música, 2001–2005
Rem Koolhaas
Oporto/Portugal

1 2 3 4 5 6 7 8 9 10 11 12 13 14 15 16 17 18 19 20 21 22 23 24 25 26 27 28 29 30 31

DECEMBER

The hidden harmony is better than
that which is obvious.

Heraclitus

Château d'Azay-le-Rideau, detail of the staircase rising, 1518–1527
Azay-le-Rideau/France

1 2 3 4 5 6 7 8 9 10 11 12 13 14 15 16 17 18 19 20 21 22 23 24 25 26 27 28 29 30 31

DECEMBER

The fact is that we live in an age of
chaotic confusion, and this applies
to art as well.... This is a situation
that leads us to expect the emergence
of something great.

Hendrik Petrus Berlage

Louvre Pyramid, 1985–1989
I. M. Pei
Paris/France

1 2 3 4 5 6 7 8 9 10 11 12 13 14 15 16 17 18 19 20 21 22 23 24 25 26 27 28 29 30 31

DECEMBER

The most beautiful buildings are not
useful: a temple is no dwelling-place.

Arthur Schopenhauer

Basilica di Santa Maria del Fiore (Il Duomo), 1296–1436
Florence/Italy

1 2 3 4 5 6 7 8 9 10 11 12 13 14 15 16 17 18 19 20 21 22 **23** 24 25 26 27 28 29 30 31

DECEMBER

The fate of the architect is the strangest
of all. How often he expends his whole
soul, his whole heart and passion,
to produce buildings into which he
himself may never enter.

Johann Wolfgang von Goethe

Sagrada Familia, detail, 1883–1926
Antoni Gaudí
Barcelona/Spain

1 2 3 4 5 6 7 8 9 10 11 12 13 14 15 16 17 18 19 20 21 22 23 24 25 26 27 28 29 30 31

DECEMBER

If you have built castles in the air,
your work need not be lost;
that is where they should be.
Now put foundations under them.

Henry David Thoreau

Sky Bridge between the Petronas Twin Towers, 1996–2003
César Pelli
Kuala Lumpur/Malaysia

1 2 3 4 5 6 7 8 9 10 11 12 13 14 15 16 17 18 19 20 21 22 23 24 25 26 27 28 29 30 31

DECEMBER

The goal is to provoke sceneries
beyond the architectural discipline –
a stage.

GRAFT

Hotel Q!, interior view, 2002–2004
GRAFT Gesellschaft von Architekten
Berlin/Germany

1 2 3 4 5 6 7 8 9 10 11 12 13 14 15 16 17 18 19 20 21 22 23 24 25 26 27 28 29 30 31

DECEMBER

There will never be great architects or
great architecture without great patrons.

Edwin Lutyens

Sanssouci, 1745–1747
Georg Wenzeslaus von Knobelsdorff
Potsdam/Germany

1 2 3 4 5 6 7 8 9 10 11 12 13 14 15 16 17 18 19 20 21 22 23 24 25 26 27 28 29 30 31

DECEMBER

Architecture is a small piece of this human
equation, but for those of us who practice it,
we believe in its potential to make a difference,
to enlighten and to enrich the human
experience, to penetrate the barriers of
misunderstanding and provide a beautiful
context for life's drama.

Frank O. Gehry

Basilica di San Marco, west façade, 829–1500
Venice/Italy

1 2 3 4 5 6 7 8 9 10 11 12 13 14 15 16 17 18 19 20 21 22 23 24 25 26 27 28 29 30 31

DECEMBER

Great architects always break with the
situation as they find it…. There were
always radical moments of change,
moments in which something different
became visible.

Peter Eisenman

Johnson Wax Research Tower, 1944–1950
Frank Lloyd Wright
Racine/USA

1 2 3 4 5 6 7 8 9 10 11 12 13 14 15 16 17 18 19 20 21 22 23 24 25 26 27 28 29 30 31

DECEMBER

I believe that architecture today needs
to reflect on the tasks and possibilities
which are inherently its own.
Architecture is not a vehicle or a
symbol for things that do not belong
to its essence.

Peter Zumthor

The Royal Pavilion, 1815–1822
John Nash
Brighton/England

1 2 3 4 5 6 7 8 9 10 11 12 13 14 15 16 17 18 19 20 21 22 23 24 25 26 27 28 29 30 31

DECEMBER

Index

Photo Credits

US Capitol Building 6/20, 7/6
Wies, Wies Church 3/14
Wilford, Michael & Partners 3/17, 5/27
Wilford, Stirling, Nägeli 10/21
Wolfsburg, Phœno Science Center 12/18
Wren, Christopher 2/18, 7/29, 12/16
Wright, Frank Lloyd 3/20, 5/2, 8/12, 12/30
Yamasaki, Minoru 10/19
Yazd, Kabir Jaame Mosque 8/16
Yucatan, Palace in Xlapak 8/24
Zaor, Jan 4/13
Zaragoza, Torre del Agua 2/16
Zimmermann, Johann Baptist and Dominikus 3/14
Zumthor, Peter 4/8, 6/4

The photos in this book were kindly made available by laif agentur für photos und reportagen: Adenis/Gaff: February 3, March 14, October 9; Almargo/Gamma: April 10; Amme: May 3; Artz: February 20; Aurora: March 20; Babovic: December 2; Back: February 23, December 27; Barbier Bruno/hemis.fr: October 6; Berthold Steinhilber: November 23; Bie Sam/Gamma/eyedea: May 12; Bock H.: June 7; Body Philippe/hemis.fr: December 8; Boening/Zenit: January 16, April 30, May 24, October 24; Boisvieux Christophe/eyedea/Hoa-qui: April 13, August 25; Borgese Maurizio/hemis.fr: March 10; Boudha/Gramma: April 21; Bruno Perousse/hemis.fr: November 26; Bungert, Sabine: January 8, April 20; Buss Wojtek/Hoa-qui/eyedea: May 16; Butzmann/Zenit: December 3; Catherine Bibollet/eyedea: February 27; Chicurel Arnaud/hemis.fr: April 18; ChinaFotoPress: April 9; Christian Cuny/Rapho/eyedea Illustration: May 21; Cintract RoMayn/hemis.fr: March 11; Clemens Emmler: February 15, July 19; Contrasto: January 4, March 9, April 26, July 4, 21, 24, August 29, October 1, 4, 28, November 11; Dagmar Schwelle: February 26, August 23, November 25; Derwal Fred/hemis.fr: May 28; Digaetano/Polaris: November 8; Dozier Marc/hemis.fr: March 4, 5, April 6, 29, June 18, July 1, August 27, November 30, December 13, 21; Dugast J.-T./eyedea: June 15; Eddie Gerald: April 5; Eitan Simanor/Hoa-qui/eyedea Illustration: November 19; Emile Luider/Rapho: October 25, November 20; Escudero Patrick/hemis.fr: May 22, October 11; Eslami Rad/Gamma/eyedea Presse: August 16; François Gohier/Hoa-qui/eyedea Illustration: November 18; Frank Heuer: February 17; Fred. Thomas/Hoa-qui/eyedea Illustration: July 22, August 19, September 11, October 20, 22, November 12, 20; Frieder Blickle: January 26; Frumm John/hemis.fr: April 25, October 5, 17; Galli: January 7, 15, February 11, March 7, 27, April 4, 28, May 27, August 11, September 14, November 3, 4; Galliarde Raphael/Gamma/eyedea Presse:

May 29; Gaasterland: May 13; Gamma/eyedea Presse: June 14; Gardel Bertrand/hemis.fr: May 26, December 23, 26; Gernot Huber: April 8; Gilles Rigoulet/hemis.fr: May 17, August 10, September 16, 21; Gonzalez: June 1, August 14; Guiziou Franck/hemis.fr: January 6, 17, 24, August 28; Hahn: March 16; Heeb: January 10, February 28/29, April 3, June 23, 30, November 10, 24, December 16; Heiko Meyer: June 10, October 21; Hemis: January 13, February 19, 5, 8, 9, 14, 25, March 8, 13, 24, April 1, May 14, 19, June 20, 25, 29, July 5, 7, 18, 23, 27, August 2, 5, 8, 17, 22, 26, September 10, 19, October 27, November 7, 27, 28, December 4; Hemispheres: January 9, 21, 31, February 2, 4, 12, March 23, 31, April 27, May 30, June 5, 26, 27, July 20, August 9, 12, September 18, 25, 28, October 12, December 29; Hervé Champollion/eyedea/Top: March 21, August 12, October 30; Herve Hughes/hemis.fr: February 16, August 15, September 24, November 2, December 12; Hoa-Qui: May 9, 31, June 6, August 6, September 22, November 14; Holland. Hoogte: August 31; Horst Dieter Zinn: September 23; Horst Kloever: July 15; IML: May 25, December 24; Jacques Sierpinski/Top/eyedea Illustration: October 16; Jalain Francis/Hoa-qui: December 25; Jan-Peter Boening/Zenit: October 3; Jean-Claude Varga/Keystone-Franc: January 5, July 9; Jean-Daniel Sudres/eyedea: February 24; Jean-Pierre Couraeu/eystone-France/Explorere Archives/eyedea Presse: August 24; Joubert Jean-Denis/Hoa-qui/eyedea Illustration: September 8; Katja Hoffmann: February 18, March 15, December 5; Kirchgessner: February 1, December 9; Kirchner: March 28, April 2, 14, 15, June 9, August 20, 30, November 15; Klein: March 2, July 3; Krinitz: September 26; November 26; Kristensen: August 4; Kurt Henseler: October 15; laif: June 19, October 7; Langrock: April 12; Le Figaro Magazine: January 25, February 10, July 28, October 8; Lescourret JP/Explorer/

eyedea/Hoa-qui: June 8, 11, July 6, September 12; Linkel: October 14; Lorenzo Ciniglio/Polaris: September 1; Maysant Ludovic/hemis.fr: January 28, March 17, April 16, May 5, 20, June 28, September 3, December 15; Manousos Daskalogiannis/IML: October 23; Marc Gantier/Rapho/eyedea Illustration: October 26; Marcus Hoehn: May 18; Mattes René/hemis.fr: January 18, 30, April 24, July 12, 25, November 9; Mattes R./Hoa-qui/Explorer/eyedea Illustration: September 7; Maurizio Borgese/hemis.fr: January 14; Michael Martin: January 1; Moirenc Camille/hemis.fr: April 11, October 2; Morandi Bruno/hemis.fr: July 14, 30, September 4, 6, 15, October 18, December 7; Patrick Escudero/hemis.fr: March 18, August 21; Patrick Forget/eyedea/Hoa-qui: March 6, April 19, September 20; Patrick Forget/Explorer/Hoa-qui/eyedea Illustration: October 10; Patrick Frilet/hemis.fr: November 17; Paul Langrock/Zenit: November 21; Paul Spierenburg: February 21, September 13; Perkovic: January 23, April 23, September 5; Philippe Roy/Hoa-qui/eyedea Illustration : October 29, November 14; Piel Patrick/Gamma/eydea: February 22; Piepenburg: January 2; Pierre-Olivier Deschamps/VU: January 12, December 18; Putelat Pierre/Hoa-qui/eyedea Illustration: July 2; Raach: January 3; Rapho: April 17, July 11, August 18, November 16; REA: January 11, March 22, November 1, December 22; REA/Financial Times: July 29; Regina Bermes: July 16; Reinicke: June 22; Reporters: July 26; Rieger Bertrand/hemis.fr: December 19; Riehle: March 3, December 6; Robert Tixador/eyedea/Top: March 12, May 23; Rodtmann: September 9; Sasse: May 2, September 27; Seux Paule/hemis.fr: April 22, September 17; Steets: June 21, November 5; Stefan Falke: February 13; Stuart Forster/TCS: February 19; Sylvain Grandadam/Hoa-qui/eyedea Illustration: May 15; TCS: June 12; The NewYork-Times/Redux: January 20, 27, June 16, July 10; Thomas Linkel: February 6;

Thouvenin Guy/Hoa-qui/Explorer/eyedea Illustration: December 10; Tobias Gerber: July 8, September 2; Tony Law/Redux: July 31; Top: May 8; Tophoven: August 3; VU: February 7, March 30, April 7, May 7, June 4, November 13; Westrich: January 29; Wysocki Pawel/hemis.fr: May 4; Yang Fuzeng/ChinaFotoPress: March 1; Yann Guichaoua/eyedea/Hoa-qui: March 26, May 10, June 24, October 13; Zanettini: August 1
Further images are taken from: Achim Bednorz, Cologne: December 1; akg-images/Hervé Champollion: March 25; akg-images/Bildarchiv Monheim: December 11; all over/Marcus Brooke: November 6; artur: December 20; Bilderberg, Hamburg/Reinhart Wolf: June 17; Corbis/Vince Streano: August 7; Esto/Esra Stoller: December 30; Foster + Partners: March 19; Georges Fessy: December 14; IFA, Munich, /Fritz Schmid: December 31; Jörg Machirus/Mac-Fotoservice: September 29, October 31, December 17; Look: May 1, November 22; Look/Jürgen Richter: May 1; Mark Fiennes: June 13; Markus Hilbich: March 29, September 30; Nigel Young/Foster + Partners: January 22; Norman McGrath: May 11; Rainer Kiedrowski: July 17; Scala, Florenz: July 13; Scott Murphy: October 19

Spine: see August 2
Back cover: see January 1, August 12, June 1, September 4